PENGUIN BUSINESS
HOW BUSINESS STORYTELLING WORKS

Sandeep Das has been a corporate leader for nearly fifteen years, having worked as Director at PricewaterhouseCoopers (PwC), Accenture Strategy, Marico and BCG. He is currently the Global Foresight Lead for Emerging Countries for Mars Wrigley.

He is the author of *Hacks for Life and Career: A Millennial's Guide to Making It Big*, *Yours Sarcastically* and *Satan's Angels*. His books have been featured in *Fortune*, the *Times of India*, the *Economic Times*, *Mint*, *Deccan Chronicle*, *Business Line*, *The Asian Age*, CNN IBN, *The Hindu*, *Bangalore Mirror* and *Mid-Day*.

He is a popular columnist with *Fortune*, *Forbes*, the *Times of India*, the *Economic Times*, *Mint* and *Businessworld*, having written over 150 columns for them. He has been quoted extensively by *Fortune*, *Mint*, Moneycontrol, *Deccan Chronicle* and the *Financial Express*, among other publications.

He has been invited as a guest speaker at more than 100 leading corporates and institutes. He has spoken at corporates such as the Tata Group, Indian Oil, Tata Consultancy Services (TCS), Bajaj Electricals, upGrad, Deloitte, Accenture and PwC. Some of the institutes Sandeep has spoken at are the National University of Singapore (NUS), IIM Bangalore, IIM Calcutta, IIT Bombay, IIT Delhi and St Stephen's College, Delhi.

His videos on YouTube have been watched over a million times. His posts on LinkedIn have been seen over 10 million times.

By education, he is an MBA from IIM Bangalore and has completed a strategy course from INSEAD.

ADVANCE PRAISE

'Action-packed and entertaining, as a book on storytelling should be! Fresh examples from across the globe, backed by solid science. I loved it.'

Dr Zoe Chance,
Yale University, Author of
Influence Is Your Superpower

'Storytelling is a critical life skill that everyone must try to learn. Who else could one go to but the master storyteller Sandeep Das? I had the fortune of observing his storytelling magic from very close quarters—for instance how he convinced the chairman of a large conglomerate on how he needed to review his business differently. Go and turn the pages of his latest work to experience his storytelling charm first-hand. You won't be disappointed.'

Tarun Satiya,
Managing Director, Accenture Strategy

'Sandeep Das is a strong new voice among the next generation of leadership thinkers and speakers. You should pay attention to the stories he tells. Read every word. And if you get the chance to actually hear him speak, drop everything and get there if you can. He will open your mind.'

Steven Sonsino,
Business School Professor and Bestselling Author

'Sandeep's book beautifully captures the essence of business storytelling in an era of unfinished stories.'

Prasad Sangameshwaran,
Editor, BrandEquity.com at
The Economic Times

'Finally a book which lays out a practical and grounded approach to how we can all benefit from the power of storytelling in our lives. A must-read for anyone who desires to demystify the concept and use it.'

Sunit Sinha,
Partner and Head—People,
Performance and Culture at KPMG India

'What I love about this book is that it brings out interesting takeaways from the world of movies, behavioural psychology and human evolution into our day-to-day corporate lives. This book is a must-read for all corporates who are interested in learning about the skill of storytelling.'

Prateek Mathur,
Vice President and Head, Reliance Retail

'In this book, Sandeep explains how you can harness the power of stories for effective communication, be it in your own life or for the business you lead. Replete with interesting anecdotes and backed by science and research, this book is thoroughly enjoyable and richly insightful.'

Sourav Mukherji,
Professor and Dean (Alumni Relations
and Development), IIM Bangalore

HOW BUSINESS STORYTELLING WORKS

Increase Your Influence and Impact

SANDEEP DAS

BUSINESS

An imprint of Penguin Random House

PENGUIN BUSINESS

USA | Canada | UK | Ireland | Australia
New Zealand | India | South Africa | China | Singapore

Penguin Business is part of the Penguin Random House group of companies
whose addresses can be found at global.penguinrandomhouse.com

Published by Penguin Random House India Pvt. Ltd
4th Floor, Capital Tower 1, MG Road,
Gurugram 122 002, Haryana, India

Penguin
Random House
India

First published in Penguin Business by Penguin Random House India 2023

ISBN 9780143461951

Typeset in Sabon by Fidus Design Pvt Ltd, Chandigarh.
Printed at Gopsons Papers Pvt. Ltd., Noida

www.penguin.co.in

MIX
Paper from
responsible sources
FSC® C191020

To Mom, Dad, Dadu and Dida
for everything
they have done for me.

CONTENTS

LIST OF FIGURES

LIST OF ABBREVIATIONS

ASMR	Autonomous sensory meridian response
BTS	Bangtan Sonyeondan
CFO	Chief financial officer
CHRO	Chief human resources officer
CIO	Chief information officer
CMO	Chief marketing officer
COO	Chief operating officer
COVID-19	Coronavirus Disease 2019
CXO	Chief experience officer
H&M	Hennes and Mauritz
HR	Human resources
IHG	InterContinental Hotels Group PLC
IIM	Indian Institute of Management
IIT	Indian Institute of Technology
MBA	Master of Business Administration
MILE	Mass interactive live events
MLB	Major League Baseball
MTR	Mavalli Tiffin Room
NBA	National Basketball Association
NFT	Non-fungible token
NPS	Net Promoter Score

NUS	National University of Singapore
PSG	Paris Saint-Germain
PwC	PricewaterhouseCoopers
SAS	Scandinavian Airlines System
SEC	Securities and Exchange Commission
TCS	Tata Consultancy Services
TED	Technology, Entertainment, Design
VR	Virtual reality
WWE	World Wrestling Entertainment

FOREWORD

When I went through formal management education 30 years ago, the focus was on logic, analytical skills and rigour. Our marketing professor would interrupt any student who prefaced his comments with 'I feel that....' The mind was expected to lead the heart.

Today, we realize that a successful leader needs much more than analysis. They need to be able to tell stories to rally the troops. A product or brand needs to be accompanied by a powerful story for it to be successful in the marketplace. An entrepreneur needs to have an engaging story to persuade an investor to take a stake in their enterprise. Storytelling has become an important skill in business.

I have known Sandeep Das since he was a student in my Master of Business Administration (MBA) strategy class 15 years ago. I have watched him chart his career as a speaker, author and consultant. He was a good storyteller back then but is even better now!

This is a timely and useful book on business storytelling. Sandeep makes a strong case for why storytelling is important. Storytelling is an art, but Sandeep has synthesized insights from diverse sources to create a guide to effective storytelling.

This book is wide in scope, with tips on how to become a master storyteller in a range of individual and business contexts. It is practical yet rides on a foundation of strong concepts. Sandeep has practised the principles he preaches in the way he has written them, with excellent examples and an informal and engaging style. I learnt a lot from reading it, I am sure you will too.

Rishikesha T. Krishnan
Director and Professor of Strategy
Indian Institute of Management Bangalore

PREFACE
Hmmm... Why Exactly Should You Read This Book?

So you have either bought this book or are considering buying this book by reading this preface. Bear with me and read the next few pages before you decide to drop this book and watch the latest Instagram reel instead.

Before I make my elevator pitch for reading this book, let me ask you a question.

Who do you think is the greatest storyteller of all time?

Take a minute before you answer. Do not come up with multiple answers. Narrow down and come up with just one name. Just one.

I have done this exercise at many storytelling workshops. Their answers and hopefully yours will revolve primarily around the following names:

- Barack Obama
- Narendra Modi
- Steve Jobs
- Aaron Sorkin
- Sheryl Sandberg
- Elon Musk
- Christopher Nolan
- Indra Nooyi
- Johnny Depp

THE #1 SKILL YOU NEED

It is quite obvious to say that there is a lot of NOISE around us, with so many advertisements, social media feeds, toxic bosses, nosy relatives, irritating friends who seem to be leading the perfect life, so many pundits jumping up and down trying to motivate you by selling something to you and so on (refer Figure P.1).

It is also obvious that the world, after the pandemic, is changing faster than ever before. There was talk of 100 per cent remote work, which was followed by a hybrid working model that will evolve into something else by the time this book has reached your hand. We are ridiculously divided as a population, ready to unleash a torrential wave of hatred and pounce on each other. There are millions of us trying to be influencers. There are millions of us trying to be entrepreneurs.

In this complicated world, the single biggest facet that is lacking is trust and authenticity. Everyone is trying to sell amid so much noise. One of India's leading advertising moguls, Prasoon Joshi, recently mentioned that the biggest quality that is required between a creator and an audience is trust.[1] Do not think that a creator only means a social media influencer. A creator stands for everyone—an entrepreneur, a corporate professional, a marketing head, a student or an author.

---

[1] Do you agree with what he is saying? The link to the interview: https://timesofindia.indiatimes.com/entertainment/hindi/bollywood/news/prasoon-joshi-the-biggest-thing-is-the-trust-between-the-creator-and-the-audience/articleshow/87239873.cms

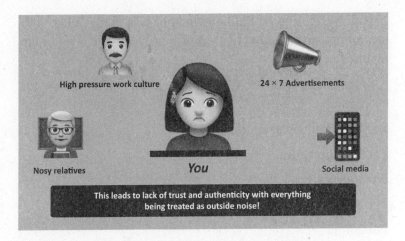

Figure P.1: Why You Have Trust Issues in Life

Storytelling, as a tool, helps you bridge that critical gap by sounding authentic and building that missing level of trust. As someone who does marketing and understands human psychology during the hours of the day, the single biggest human insight over this upcoming decade is the need for authenticity and trust.

Well, you might be thinking if storytelling is really that important or if it is just another fancy tool to have by your side. Consider these two examples:

One of the biggest reasons why Hillary Clinton lost the 2016 United States presidential election is because she was perceived to be stiff and not authentic.

I wrote an opinion piece for a leading newspaper on why tennis superstar Novak Djokovic is not loved as much as Roger Federer or Rafael Nadal. In one line, I summarized the entire story as follows:

Novak is trying to be Batman when he is actually Joker.[2] His lack of perceived authenticity is primarily why he is not a fan favourite.

Is storytelling only for CEOs? No, it isn't. It is meant for everyone:

For corporate professionals

For entrepreneurs

For sports stars

For brands and marketers

For actors

For sales professionals

For Gen Z professionals looking for their first job

For chief experience officers (CXOs) trying to pitch for the CEO's job

For aspiring politicians trying to get the president's job

Even for a terrorist trying to create global havoc

For authors like me

For professors teaching in business schools

And, finally and most importantly, for you!

In fact, storytelling helps you deal with friends and those nasty relatives. Although I am not sure whether story-telling can land you your dream date, I wouldn't rule it out either.

---

[2] The link to my article on what Novak should do to be as adored as Federer or Nadal. My suggestion is highly controversial. I recommend that he acts like a villain. https://brandequity.economictimes.indiatimes.com/news/marketing/the-curious-case-of-novak-djokovic/87728844

If you take a view over thousands of years and we discuss this in a subsequent chapter, the reason you and I have survived the hazardous journey of human evolution is our ability to tell stories. We have survived over every other species because we could create artificial mythical stories like the notion of countries, religion and corporates.

Please don't conclude that I don't believe in God. I do, especially when my increments at work are not up to the mark.

WHAT IS A STORY?

As a good or a rather bad storyteller, I am introducing the concept of a story after I have told you why it is so important.

A story is what your grandmother narrated to you when you were younger. It often had the construct, once upon a time … there was this monster … trying to create a problem … then there was this great hero … who fought against all odds … and beat the monster.

For the nerds out there, and I am sure there are quite a few, a story can be summarized in the following format:

<Conflict> followed by <struggle> followed by <resolution>

We will consider this in detail in a subsequent chapter to understand how your favourite movies and web series are written in the above format.

WHO IS SANDEEP DAS?

In case you haven't figured it out, I am referring to myself, the author of this book. The reason you should read this book is not because I am a great storyteller, but because I have done this every day at my place of work for the last 15 years. I have been trained in business storytelling and have studied human insight and behavioural psychology for a long, long time. During my leadership role in management consulting, I used to interact with CEOs every day and have picked up nuances of good and bad storytelling from them. This book is replete with those interesting anecdotes.

I have spoken about business storytelling on over 100 platforms with leading CXOs across the Tata Group, Godrej, Tata Consultancy Services, Deloitte, Accenture Strategy, PwC, and so on, and to the best management students across the National University of Singapore, the famed Indian Institutes of Technology (IITs) and the Indian Institutes of Management (IIMs). And I have written over a hundred opinion pieces in leading publications such as the *Economic Times*, *The Times of India*, *Fortune* and *Forbes* on some of these nuances.

Also, if you have read my previous book, *Hacks for Life and Career: A Millennial's Guide to Making it Big*, you are probably a fan already. I do like showing off my humility.

GET THE MOST OUT OF THIS BOOK

This book is not about academic frameworks but real-world applications of storytelling techniques irrespective of whether you are an entrepreneur, a brand manager, a Gen Z professional, a corporate sales professional, a CEO, a movie star or a TikTok influencer. It gives you a real-life primer that your peers are currently using now. Trust me, they are.

As shown in Figure P.2, this book is divided into three primary sections. The first section sets up the foundation, the second section delves into the application of storytelling for corporates and the third section aids in your personal growth.

This book is divided into 14 easy-to-read chapters, excluding this preface, with loads of contemporary and popular culture

Foundational: Understanding storytelling	Storytelling for Corporates	Storytelling for Personal Growth
Why storytelling is the #1 reason you are here today?	Driving change	Creating brilliant presentations
How does your brain react to storytelling?	Becoming a visionary entrepreneur	Making elements stick
How does Hollywood use storytelling?	Creating legendary consumer brands	Leveraging humour
Our world in the next few years	Driving corporate B2B sales	Becoming a master orator
		Excelling in interviews
		Creating your personal brand

Figure P.2: What Can You Expect in This Book? Don't You Like the Cute Chapter Names?

examples. If I were you, I would read 2–3 chapters every weekend and wrap the book up in 30–45 days. And then post on social media what you loved about this book.[3] Needless to say, given the highly entertaining writer that I am, I am quite sure you will go faster than that!

So sit back and enjoy...

---

[3] All the illustrative slides in this book have been created using Keynote software. There are nearly 50 illustrative slides in this book. I know, I am so hard working!

ACKNOWLEDGEMENTS

Without any doubt, this is my BRAVEST book. Exploring an exotic concept like storytelling by deriving storytelling principles from human evolution, behavioural psychology and the world of movies and then using these principles to find numerous applications in our professional lives is seriously daunting.

In hindsight, I think that God has blessed me with immense luck and self-belief that I could even think of pulling this off. I am grateful to you, almighty, first of all.

I have a lot of people to THANK for helping me finish my fourth book and encouraging me along the way. Without a doubt, Mom and Dad, for having supported me in whatever I have wanted to do. A special thanks to my editors Manish Kumar and Manisha Mathews—they are excellent editors. Their timely inputs, infinite patience to tolerate my stupidity and sheer knowledge have pushed the book up by many notches

Finally, thanks to everyone who read a few chapters along the way and gave me their valuable and not-so-valuable feedback.

PART 1

UNDERSTANDING STORYTELLING

What is the #1 reason you are alive today?

What is the #1 reason you will be alive tomorrow?

How does storytelling impact your brain?

How does Hollywood use storytelling?

How will storytelling play out in our world over the next few years?

The most powerful person in the world is the storyteller. The storyteller sets the vision, values and agenda of an entire generation to come.

The legendary person who made your iPhone

Don't believe everything you hear. There are always three sides to a story, Yours, Theirs and the Truth.

Anonymous quote on the internet

CHAPTER 1

WHY IS STORYTELLING THE #1 REASON YOU ARE HERE TODAY?

How long have you been alive on this planet?

I understand this may not be the best line to start a book.

Let me reframe the question. How long do you think our species, humans or *Homo sapiens*, has been alive on this planet? (For the aspiring nerds, *Homo sapiens* means wise man in Latin.)

5,000 years?

50,000 years?

The actual answer is: in excess of 200,000 years, at least that far long and maybe much more. To put this number into perspective, the world didn't have Instagram, TikTok or the iPhone then, not even the computer and many more things.

Given their miserable lives without social media, have you wondered how they survived for so many tens of thousands of years?

After all, humans are not the fastest runners. They can't outrun a cheetah.

They don't have claws to pounce on their prey. Your pointy nails come close but not close enough. They can't hunt like a lion.

They don't swim fast enough. They can't outswim a shark.

They don't camouflage very well in the wild. They can't camouflage like a chameleon.

When I ask this question on why humans survived for so long, at storytelling workshops that I conduct, I get a variety of answers ranging from their intelligence and ability to communicate through language to curiosity to learn about nature.

While some of this may be true, the #1 reason that you are alive today and reading this book is, as the chapter name suggests, the power of storytelling.

The question is how?

CREATE AN INVINCIBLE SOCIAL STRUCTURE

A good story can hold another person's attention for a significant period of time. When you get millions of humans hooked on common stories, they tend to work together and combine their resources and intelligence to become a united cohesive pack that can easily conquer other competing species.

So if you study history, what are the biggest stories that have been narrated to your ancestors?

The two most common stories that were crafted to bring millions of humans together were religion, the story of God almighty, along with political systems.

And over the last 500 years, the concept of a nation.

And over the last 200 years, the concept of a corporate.

And over the last 50 years, the concept of a sporting club or a cult musical band.

Going forward, it is likely to be the rise of popular culture references. Think of *Squid Games*, South Korean boy band Bangtan Sonyeondan (BTS) or even the Indian cricketing franchise Chennai Super Kings.

How did the stories about religion and politics bring our ancestors together?

Religion created a set of principles and a belief in a larger-than-life persona, God to be precise, that asked people to follow a similar life and assist the poor and avoid violence, most of the time.

Religion created a story about a shared notion of values via festivals and a shared notion of prosperity to make people coordinate at scale. While I am no one to suggest if God exists or not, a conceptual God did ensure that all the followers of a particular religion (e.g., Christianity, Islam and Hinduism) tended to be nudged to behave under a common umbrella. While there were wars among religious sects and even within the followers of a particular religion, by and large, humans tended to cooperate with each other.

The other institution that assisted in bringing humans together was the concept of politics. A political party or a kingdom forced people to cooperate and coordinate with each other through stories of a political system that promised shared values and prosperity. As people believed in this notion, willingly or unwillingly, it enabled their political paymasters to charge levies, raise taxes and govern the human species. This allowed the political classes to get humans to coordinate at an unprecedented level to build bridges, roads or even monuments.

Can any other species of animals create such shared stories of religion and politics? In case they could, you would most likely not be reading this book at this point.

Think of a company like Google that employs more than 150,000 very smart people across the world. How does it get the smartest people in the world to come under one roof and work in the interest of a mythical story, the corporate entity Google? True, they pay well and have fantastic perks. But in the end, it comes down to great storytelling in terms of what Google stands for, organizing the world's information[1] and the impact it creates through its software.

If you want to read more on this evolution of the human species through storytelling, you may pick up *Sapiens* or *Homo Deus* by Yuval Noah Harari.

You get a sense now of what a good story can do. And why you are alive till now.

AGAIN ... WHAT IS A STORY?

On the internet, a story is defined as the telling of an event, either true or fictional, in such a way that the listener experiences or learns something by the fact that the story was told to that person.[2]

As your grandmother explained to you, a story is a problem followed by a struggle followed by a resolution to the problem.

A story is not necessarily oral or given as a presentation. With our ancestors, stories were depicted as cave drawings, transferred across generations orally, visually drawn on paper and written through text. You should remember that both YouTube and PowerPoint are just a few decades old. The human species has survived in excess of 200,000 years.

---

[1] Read more about Google and how it looks at search: https://www.google.com/search/howsearchworks/our-approach/

[2] Definition of a story on the internet: https://www.thewrap.com/what-story-and-where-does-it-come-32636/

Stories work because they enable humans to connect with each other and be a part of the community. Remember, humans are social animals and have a deep longing to connect and be part of a community. Stories help with that.

One of the greatest sporting stories is what happened at the 2022 Australian Open final.

A 35-year-old tennis veteran, coming back from a career-threatening foot injury, is two sets down and is on the verge of defeat in the third set against the future World No. 1 Daniil Medvedev. The Australian Open has been particularly unkind to him as he has lost 4 out of the 5 finals he has played on that surface. From the moment where the win predictor gave him a mere 4 per cent chance of winning, Rafael Nadal went on to script the most amazing turnaround to lift the Australian Open and be the first male player to win 21 Grand Slams.

Why does this real-life story work so well and capture our collective imagination?

In Nadal's victory, we experience sadness, joy and the everlasting feeling of hope. It helps us to be a part of his world which we haven't been in. It helps us feel the pain of his career-threatening foot injury. It helps us feel despair when he loses the second set, in the final, which he should have won. It helps us lose a bit of hope knowing the Australian Open has been particularly unkind to him, with him losing 4 out of the 5 finals till now. But somewhere, there is also a sense of hope that probably Nadal can win it back. And in his victory, we hope that his joy will pass onto our lives. We feel a particular sense of connection and belonging when Nadal lifts that Grand Slam.

And that is a very powerful story that life has written. But is this connection just emotions or is there something deeper?

EVERYTHING IS ABOUT CHEMICALS

If a story has such a powerful impact on us, there has to be a chemical response to it in our brains. Without powerful chemicals getting released and getting us hooked, there is no way a story can have such a great impact on us.

In the brilliant Technology, Entertainment, and Design (TED) Talk on 'The Magical Science of Storytelling' given by David Phillips, he talks about how an experiment was conducted by buying 200 items on eBay for US$129 and a story was added to each of these items, resulting in the items getting resold on eBay for US$8000 dollars. Notice the magical uplift of nearly 62 times just by adding a story to each of these items.

In particular, a horse's head was bought for 99 cents and sold for 62.95 dollars. That is the raw power of storytelling.

So what are the chemicals that are released in response to a good story? What happened to your brain when you read through the Rafael Nadal story?

A good thriller story with loads of suspense leads to the release of the hormone dopamine, which is associated with focus, motivation and memory. Think of how you get absorbed when the popular 'whodunnit' murder series is on air. That is dopamine driving your focus.

When you go to a stand-up comedy show, you laugh hilariously at the concocted stories of the comedian. You are under the influence of the happiness booster hormone endorphins.

When you watch a story about a lead character struggling through his life to make both ends meet (e.g., the movie *The Pursuit of Happyness* where a father desperately tries to provide a better life for his son despite having no job or a place to stay), you release oxytocin as a love hormone that makes you feel empathy for the protagonist.

When you are going through a painful appraisal of your past year's performance and your boss is trying to build a narrative story about your non-performance, your brain is emitting the stress hormone cortisol. It is telling you to 'fight or flight' this appraisal discussion which might get you fired.

A good story, in its essence, releases a combination of carbon, hydrogen, oxygen and nitrogen. All great narratives are about these chemicals.

In Nadal's story, your brain released dopamine, oxytocin and endorphin. There might have been a bit of cortisol too in case you decided to switch off your TV set.

STORYTELLING IN TODAY'S WORLD

Over the last two centuries, the concept of nation or nationalism has taken over our lives. People take pride in the country they come from. Smart politicians create a story about their nations (e.g., the American values, Chinese communism and Cuban governance) and use that as an overarching framework to nudge human beings to behave the way they want. Because this story of a nation is so powerful, humans in these nations are ready to give up their lives for the concept of the 'nation' as a story. A war veteran, who might have lost his legs, will be proud that he sacrificed to protect the ultimate story—his nation.

Some will argue that this story of a nation, religion or politics is good in a way. It helps people mobilize together and makes them stay in peace and harmony. But never underestimate the power of a story to do devastating harm. In the modern-day world, storytelling about nationalism is also leading to hyper-jingoism and a polarized atmosphere globally. When a politician senses that he/she is losing control internally, he or she often creates a story about an external enemy and tries to attack the outsider.

One of the world's greatest evils, terrorism, attracts gullible youth across the world under the story of God calling them or the promise of luxury in heaven.

In our modern-day lives, the corporate that we work for is also the ultimate story. When a company creates a narrative of 'Don't be evil', the story resonates with hundreds of thousands of smart engineers across the world, and they decide to put all their energies together to make more money for Google.

Similarly for Facebook. Similarly for Tesla. Similarly for Unilever. Similarly for Infosys.

There are brands that create stories under the name of 'purpose' to build a community of their consumers. Coca-Cola has built a story around trying to 'refresh the world' and has brought millions of consumers under the umbrella of that story.

In our lives outside of work, we all resonate with another type of story—a football club or a music band and what they stand for. Their story brings human beings from across different cultures and geographies under the same roof. There is a beautiful story that is narrated about football superstar Lionel Messi growing up through the ranks at Barcelona and his name being synonymous with the club. Even after his move to Paris Saint-Germain (PSG), try telling a Barcelona fan in Mexico that Lionel Messi is a bad footballer. And see his or her reaction.

And let's not get into the madness behind the South Korean pop music bands. Or how influencers are becoming superstars by tapping into the 'stories' on Instagram or TikTok. No one understands the power of stories better than the big technology platforms. And they are using it brilliantly to release the right set of chemicals in your brain to keep you hooked.

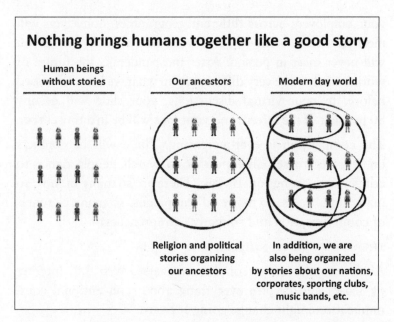

Figure 1.1: How Storytelling Brings Human Beings Together

In case it wasn't clear, religion, nationalism and political stories still work today. And probably better than other stories. Open the election manifesto of any political party, and there is bound to be a reference to religion or nationalism. The logic is simple— why change a formula that has survived through thousands of years of human evolution?

As shown in Figure 1.1, these stories unite and divide people even in this modern-day world. They will continue to do so for hundreds of thousands of years later. Some of them will be dangerous. Some won't be.

AGAIN ... THE #1 SKILL YOU NEED

It is important to understand how the next decade is likely to pan out. You are likely to work with customers, vendors and your employers across different geographies. Some you will meet physically. Some you will work with virtually. Some you will never meet in person. After the pandemic, the future of work is likely to be very different from what we have witnessed before. In your virtual discussions, your slide will occupy 80 per cent of the screen, and your face will be in a tiny corner.

The competition is ever-increasing. There will be conflicts on whether to sell shampoo or to watch people dance to cringeworthy songs on TikTok. There are so many brands, so many influencers, so many ad campaigns, so many channels of communication and so many entrepreneurs.

THERE IS SO MUCH NOISE.

Also, with the advent of the metaverse, Web 3.0, Internet of Senses and crypto, everything about conventional communication might change going forward.

No one has an attention span of more than a few seconds. Not just Generation Z but even the millennial generation or the baby boomer generation.

Hence, if you need to stand out amidst this noise—as an entrepreneur, as a marketer, as a writer, as a politician, as a digital consultant, as a recruiter, as an influencer, as a student or in any other profession, you need to learn to be a good storyteller. This is especially important as the world changes dramatically over the next 10 years.

To be honest, there are enough courses in the market, offered by universities, on storytelling. And there are other books on storytelling. However, this book with its overwhelming emphasis on being a practitioner's guide will help you get started on this journey.

So you can either master storytelling or grow a pair of horns to survive in this animalistic modern world. It is completely your choice. Not that there is much of it.

I have discovered what is wrong with my brain—on the left side, there is nothing right and on the right side, there is nothing left.

Anonymous on the internet

My brain—it is my second favourite organ.

Woody Allen, American comedian

CHAPTER 2

HOW DOES YOUR BRAIN REACT TO STORYTELLING?

In 2016, I had a deep desire to climb Mount Kilimanjaro, the highest mountain in Africa. Besides promising to be an experience of a lifetime, it was bound to get me spectacular likes on Instagram. Given such a massive journey, I needed to take permission from my family. I started the conversation by stating that only 25 people have died while climbing Mount Kilimanjaro during a period of 8 years.[1]

What do you think happened next?

***

How does the sexiest organ in your body react to storytelling? I am referring to the human brain.

When we look at the concept of storytelling and its applications, the reason this chapter gets so much traction in workshops I conduct is because of how the human brain is wired. More importantly, you as a storyteller should understand how the sexiest organ in your audience's body operates, along with its whims and fancies.

---

[1] Do you want to climb Mount Kilimanjaro? I found this statistic on the internet. http://wodocs.com/docum/1474-international_society_for_mountain_medicine-viwcmm_abstracts-32.html

To start with, as I explained in the previous chapter, stories lead to various chemicals being released in the brain. Hence, the stickiness factor of a good or a bad story can affect your brain. A good thrilling story that drives focus releases dopamine. A good set of jokes from concocted stories by a stand-up comedian releases endorphins. A story where you empathize with the protagonist releases oxytocin. A story about how you suck in life releases cortisol.

Let's read about some interesting theories of how the human brain operates and what it means for you as a storyteller. I should tell you that there are a million theories explored around the human brain. I will touch upon the ones I think will help you the most as a storyteller.

EVOLUTION SUGGESTS THE END MATTERS

Suppose you were to go through an intensely irritating procedure called colonoscopy. If you are not familiar with this procedure, a long tube with a camera is sent up your backside to view the inside of your colon. Let me give you two scenarios and ask which one you would prefer.

Scenario 1: Ten minutes of colonoscopy which is highly irritating, say a 7 on a pain scale of 1–10 where 10 is the maximum

Scenario 2: Fifteen minutes of colonoscopy which is a combination of 10 minutes of irritating pain on a scale of 7 out of 10 and the last 5 minutes as a dummy exercise where the tube is largely pulled outside, and so the irritation is 2 out of 10.

Which scenario would you prefer? Any logical person would prefer Scenario 1 as the pain borne is 70 units (10 minutes × 7 units of pain), whereas in Scenario 2, the pain borne is 80 units (10 minutes × 7 units of pain + 5 minutes × 2 units of pain)

You might be astonished to realize that the human brain prefers Scenario 2.

This is technically explained by the peak-end theory that was discovered and explored by Dr Daniel Kahneman,[2] a Nobel Prize-winning Israeli psychologist. In simple English, what he proved was that the human brain measured an overall experience by how it ended and the peak moments during that experience rather than the overall duration of the experience. The human brain provides lower importance to the start of the experience but provides tremendous importance to the end of the experience. This is one of the reasons why women report a favourable experience of their overall pregnancy despite it being long for 9 months, painful and irritating due to the intense rush of positive hormones at the end. There are numerous experiments conducted to prove this theory.[3]

Sounds weird, isn't it? But it isn't actually.

If you are a sports fan, what do you remember about the 2011 cricket world cup? Many of you will say M. S. Dhoni hitting the final six. Do you remember that Gautam Gambhir was the top scorer during the final with a blistering 97?

If you are a tennis fan, what do you like about Novak Djokovic? A lot of you might say his ability to never give up and fight back from match points at the end. I am quite sure you remember the Wimbledon 2019 final where Roger Federer lost the iconic Grand Slam after failing to close the match in spite of having two match points on his serve in the fifth set. People often remember how Novak has won many matches after being a match point down.

If you like the movie *The Sixth Sense*, an American psychological supernatural thriller starring Bruce Willis, what do

---

[2] For an easier explanation on the topic, https://positivepsychology.com/what-is-peak-end-theory/

[3] For the interested reader, you may read Thinking Fast and Slow by Daniel Kahneman himself.

you like about it? Many of you might say the ending where Bruce Willis realizes he has been dead all along.

Why did people like the *Batman* series by Christopher Nolan? If you traverse the internet, the reviews are around the twists in the movies, the iconic lines and the ending. Especially at the end, when Christian Bale aka Batman turns out to be alive as he eats in the same restaurant as his caretaker, Alfred.

What do children like about a birthday party? You might hear answers about when they danced, what they ate and behold, the return gift at the end.

If you go to a restaurant that doesn't serve great food but it ends with your favourite dessert, you might judge the overall experience less harshly.

If you go to a musical concert where the equipment isn't great but the band plays your favourite song at the end, you might judge the overall experience favourably.

To be honest, the fact that the brain looks at the ending as the most important aspect of an experience along with a few peak points along the way shouldn't be rocket science. Movie script writers knew about this decades ago, and hence, they felt the need to always have an unexpected twist at the end. Remember the movie *Psycho*, released in 1960, where it turns out that the protagonist Norman Bates murdered his mother a long time ago.

As a business, the human brain often remembers the peaks in a company's journey. If I ask you how old Apple is as a company, some of you might struggle to answer the question. It was founded in 1976.

Instead, if I ask you what your memorable moments from Apple are, some of you might say the release of the iPhone and the iPad, Steve Jobs being fired and him being brought back. Notice that the peak need not be a positive moment but can be a negative moment like Steve Jobs being asked to leave his own company.

As a storyteller, when an experience is being defined, the ending is absolutely critical and mind-blowing peaks are absolutely essential. As the subsequent chapters will show, peaks are generated by narrating stories about human beings.

When you define a consumer experience, the ending matters supremely. If you are shopping in a supermarket and have long waiting lines at the checkout, it is likely the human brain might perceive the entire experience unfavourably due to an unpleasant end. Designing the experience where the ending is perceived to be great, by making it flawless with goodies or just outperforming, goes a long way in tricking the sexiest organ in your body.

ANECDOTES OVER NUMBERS

In all my storytelling workshops, I present the following two fictional scenarios and ask participants to choose which one they are likely to remember more.

Both represent the same message.

Which one do you think if presented in a large forum, say of over 100 people, will be remembered by a greater number of members of the audience?

Scenario 1: There is a 90 per cent statistical probability that nearly 73 per cent of urban women will increase their online shopping basket by 27 per cent resulting in an e-commerce channel salience of over 30 per cent.

Scenario 2: Mehak, a 27-year-old woman working in Singapore, will buy most of her weekly groceries online from now on.

Take another minute. Which message do you think is likely to be remembered by an audience once you have presented these two scenarios?

Let me make this easy for you and show it in a visual form. Refer to Figures 2.1 and 2.2.

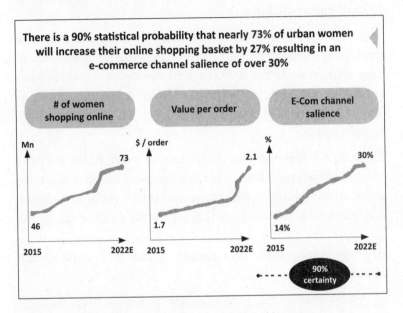

Figure 2.1: Do You Love This Scenario: 1?

Source: Nielsen consumer behaviour, expert interviews, primary research with 30 consumers

Mehak, works for an advertising agency in Singapore. She plans to make all her grocery purchases online from now on.

Figure 2.2: Do You Love This Scenario: 2?

As you might have guessed, for more people, it is likely to be Scenario 2 when the audience is very large. In the workshops I conduct, it is generally 75 per cent in favour of Scenario 2.

While some of you may protest that Scenario 1 seems more rigorous and methodical, which it is not, Scenario 2 is likely to have higher stickiness.

The root cause for this behaviour is the bias that exists in the human brain. The bias or the subconscious behaviour at play with your brain is 'Representativeness', which implies predicting the general behaviour from a specific example. You assume that the specific example is an indicator of the larger sample.

How could you use this weirdness of your brain to your natural advantage? Well, it is fairly simple. During a narrative story, always have a few powerful anecdotes that indicate a larger trend. We will see this leveraged extensively in the world of movies and in the subsequent chapters—in the form of client testimonials, user success stories and inspirational anecdotes.

In brand marketing, this principle is represented through consumer personas. For the purpose of storytelling, as an illustration, the following persona might be created for the iPhone consumer.

'Meet Aspirational Ana. She is a 25-year-old trying to make a career in an ad agency. Over the weekend, she loves photography and appreciates a good camera. She has loads of pictures on her phone and is paranoid about them being leaked through malware'.

This persona might be a narrative that is built by a marketing head to drive stickiness in internal communication. Although this persona is specific, the underlying set of data points will be numerically robust. For instance, the company might have done a study which might highlight that 86 per cent of Gen Z women who work in creative lines love a phone that has a breathtaking camera and strong security. Using this research as a base, a specific persona is built which drives stickiness with your brain.

So anecdotes on their own are very powerful. You get that. How else might you leverage powerful anecdotes? Anecdotes work very well in pairs—something that is referred to, by me, as Nested Anecdotes. Let me take you through an example.

If you were to address a large gathering on the need for resilience in life, you could start with this anecdote,

> I am going to speak about this certain cricketer. He was known to be the next big thing. In his debut match, this cricketer got zero and zero. A horrid debut to be honest. To be fair, his cricketing board still persisted with him. He was given a few more chances but somehow he couldn't make it big with those chances. Many people questioned his resilience and determination. He did fade away after some time. I am not going to take his name. But I want to talk about being resilient when things are not going in your favour.

And you could continue with your speech about being resilient during tough times and not fading away. In the end, you can bring the same anecdote back and complete it with a different twist.

> Do you remember the cricketer I spoke about when I was starting off? He was known to be the next big thing. In his debut match, this cricketer got zero and zero. A horrid debut to be honest. He was dropped. He made a comeback after 21 months. He got zero and one. He was dropped. He made a comeback after 17 months. He got zero and zero. He was dropped. He made a comeback after 36 months. This

time, Marvan Atapattu, scored 16 centuries in Test matches, 11 centuries in One Day Internationals and captained the Sri Lankan cricket team.

Why do Nested Anecdotes work? First of all, think of Nested Anecdotes as Russian dolls. Once you open one, you have to close it. Or like a computer program, once you open a loop, you have to close it. In this case, you are closing the opening anecdote. An anecdote at the beginning captures your brain. An anecdote at the end captures your attention. By providing a twist at the end, you are catering to the bias in your brain which evaluates an experience largely by the ending.

Great movies often start with the ending and build the movie from there. Think of *Memento*, *Pulp Fiction*, *The Usual Suspects* and a crime series like *How to Get Away with Murder*. In the movie *Fight Club*, one of my all-time favourites, the first scene has the protagonist, played by Edward Norton, with the gun in his mouth speaking to Tyler Durden, played by Brad Pitt, and narrating that Marla, played by Helena Carter, changed the course of his life. In the ending, the same scene is played back, and it is revealed that Brad Pitt is an alternate personality of Edward Norton.

How do you want to try Nested Anecdotes?

MAGICAL RULE OF 3

I once attended a communication workshop facilitated by an Australian expert. She mentioned that the most impactful communication is always done in sets of 3 and critical messages are delivered in blocks of 3. It was a very interesting statement that she made. Aristotle, the famous Greek philosopher, made the observation that people find it easiest to remember in groups of 3. Have you wondered why critical messages are always delivered in blocks of 3?

For instance, when you speak to the CEO of a company, he or she will always ask you, 'so what are the 3 things we should do next?'

Your favourite movie is often divided into 3 Acts and not 2 and not 5.

Think of the *Batman* franchise by Christopher Nolan; it was showcased as a trilogy like many other successful franchises.

When you are taught journalism, you are taught to present 3 main arguments while speaking or writing. It is called the 'Rule of 3'.

When Thomas Jefferson was writing about the United States Declaration of Independence, he wrote about three things— life, liberty and the pursuit of happiness.

Interestingly, the human body's survival operates on the rule of 3. It is said the human body's ability to stay alive depends on patterns of 3:3 minutes without air, 3 hours in extreme heat or cold and 3 days without water.

For the mathematics aficionados, myself included, you preferably refer to 3 standard deviations showcasing 99.7 per cent of the data, not 1 or 2 standard deviations. In case you didn't get this statement, just ignore it and move on.

The reason the number '3' becomes so important is that it is the easiest number for your brain to form patterns and remember them after that. For every number greater than 3, it is more effort intensive for your brain to remember that extra item. Lesser than 3, your brain might not identify a pattern or consider it rigorous enough.

From a storytelling perspective, this implies that you communicate three main arguments, three next steps or even three key components in a slide. Less than this is not rigorous enough for your brain. More than 3 and it becomes complex for your brain.

POP CULTURE REFERENCES RULE

Let me ask you a question.

You have read a few chapters till now. What examples that I have written about come to your mind now? Try recollecting the top 3.

When I have asked this question at workshops, examples of movies or sports stars or famous brands come to people's minds. I think yours won't be too different either.

While narrating good stories, references from popular culture work well. By popular culture, I mean examples of sportspersons, movie stars, famous entrepreneurs, characters from hit sitcoms, etc.

Following are a few stories for you to ponder over.

In case you want to communicate to someone about how short-term failure and struggles are good, you will often talk about a sportsperson and their incredible journey before they became big. Indian cricketing legend M. S. Dhoni's struggle as a ticket collector on a railway station is well documented. So is football superstar Cristiano Ronaldo's humble background while growing up. And tennis legend Roger Federer's indelible pain of losing his beloved coach, Peter Carter, at a very young age.

In case you want to communicate about persevering in the light of constant failure, you will often hear the mention of Abraham Lincoln's constant set of failures before he became the President of the United States in 1860. Following is the list of failures that egged him on to get the top job.

He lost his job in 1832.

He was defeated for state legislature in 1832.

He failed in business in 1833.

His sweetheart died in 1835.

He had a nervous breakdown in 1836.

He was defeated for Speaker in 1838.

He was defeated for nomination for the Congress in 1843.

He lost his re-nomination to the Congress in 1848.

He was rejected for land officer in 1849.

He was defeated for US Senate in 1854.

He was defeated for nomination for vice president in 1856.

He was defeated for the US Senate in 1858.

He was elected president of the United States in 1860.[4]

Another great story that is often communicated for achieving success despite all failures is the journey of Hollywood superstar Keanu Reeves. Despite his successes as part of *Speed*, *Matrix* or *John Wick* movies, he has had to endure a lot of personal losses.

At the age of 3, Keanu's father abandoned him.

He was expelled from one of his many schools. He went to four different schools in 5 years.

He lost one of his closest friends River Phoenix.

He lost his unborn child in 1999. As a result, his marriage came to an end.

His younger sister went through a painful bout of cancer.[5]

Despite him maniacally asking everyone not to target his dog in reel life in 'John Wick', life went after him with quite a vengeance in real life.

---

[4] You have to respect his resiliency in life. A chronology of his list of failures: https://www.abrahamlincolnonline.org/lincoln/education/failures.htm

[5] This man has been through a lot in his life. https://www.looper.com/395869/tragic-details-about-keanu-reeves/

In case you want to communicate about someone who had it all but threw everything away, you are often told the story of the following gentleman.

Golfing legend Tiger Woods' story is often showcased as someone who had the world at his feet personally and professionally, but his sexual antics led to his spectacular downfall in life. He was designed to be the greatest golfer of all time beating Jack Nicklaus' record of 18 majors, but his career went through a complete downward spiral after his misconducts came to light.

The moot point is that examples from popular culture resonate when you are trying to convey a larger message. While this may seem obvious, the underlying behaviour that is at play is the 'availability bias' that your brain is infected with. Availability bias refers to the ability of your brain to rely on immediate examples that readily come to it when evaluating a particular topic.

Also, the chemicals in your brain are at play. When you talk of a successful sportsperson, in your mind, he has given you joy (endorphin), thrilling matches (dopamine) and your admiration and empathy for his struggle to succeed (oxytocin).

So when you are trying to convey a message, leveraging popular culture references is the way to go. These thinking paradigms will be used extensively going forward as we look at the application of storytelling to corporate functions and your individual careers in Parts 2 and 3 of this book.

Not sure if you picked this up, but despite the magical number for communication being in groups of 3, I have given you 4 key thinking frameworks in this chapter (refer Figure 2.3).

Either I am a very bad storyteller or I am giving you more than what you paid for.

Some of you may have the question, aren't there more interesting theories about the brain? Surely, there are. Have you heard of System 1 and System 2?

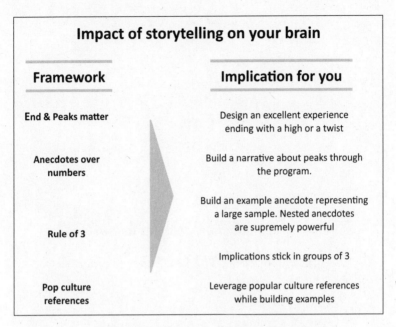

Impact of storytelling on your brain

Framework	Implication for you
End & Peaks matter	Design an excellent experience ending with a high or a twist
Anecdotes over numbers	Build a narrative about peaks through the program.
Rule of 3	Build an example anecdote representing a large sample. Nested anecdotes are supremely powerful
	Implications stick in groups of 3
Pop culture references	Leverage popular culture references while building examples

Figure 2.3: Implication of Storytelling on Your Brain

One of the most common biases in your brain is the 'Framing Effect'. It is the equivalent of saying that you prefer a product when it is communicated as '90 per cent fat-free' rather than saying it has '10 per cent fat'. Both are essentially the same.

Now if you recollect my desire to climb Mount Kilimanjaro and the horror on my family's faces when I told them that only 25 people had died during a period of 8 years. Instead, if I told them that 999,987 out of 1,000,000 climbers were alive, not successful but alive, do you think I would have had a better chance of convincing my family?

Did you realize how I just manipulated your brain? I didn't do it through framing as some of you might think. It is something else. Think again.

I am going to make him an offer he can't refuse.

Don Corleone, *The Godfather* (1972)

Let me tell you something: there's no nobility in poverty.
I've been a poor man and I've been a rich man.
And I choose rich every time.

Leonardo DiCaprio, *The Wolf of Wall Street* (2013)

CHAPTER 3

HOW DOES HOLLYWOOD USE STORYTELLING?

This might be the most interesting chapter in this book. Let me not build your hopes up unnecessarily. To reframe my statement, I had the most fun writing this chapter. And to be honest, I am quite sure you will have the most fun reading this chapter.

We all love the world of movies and TV series. They take us to a parallel world, a fantasy world, engage us and stay in our memories for eternity. The first movie that ever captured my attention was *The Shawshank Redemption*. I am not sure, but I must have seen that movie over a dozen times, picking up a new nuance every time.

The greatest stories are not told by master orators or behavioural psychologists, but by the world of movies. Without a doubt, no industry has ever captured our collective imagination like the world of movies. They release the right set of chemicals in abundance in our brains for a long period of time.

In this chapter, we will learn the common principles of storytelling from the world of movies.

The nerd in me is very proud to admit that I have gone through hundreds and hundreds of movies and web series to come up with a mathematical view of how a typical script is written.

I would never say this on a date, but this nerdy exercise has been extremely enjoyable. So wear your intellectual seat belts and come on this journey with me. It will be an extremely enriching one.

I would have said, 'May the force be with you' at this point, but I don't have the poise to say it the way they say it in *Star Wars*. But you get my intent, I am sure.

A STANDARD TEMPLATE

Figure 3.1 captures a standard template in which a movie script or a web series is written. I should say that this is not the only way to write a movie script or a web series, but this might be the most common one.

The x-axis, or the horizontal axis, represents the movement over time. The y-axis, or the vertical axis, indicates the intensity of human emotion.

Any movie or web series comprises 3 parts colloquially termed Act 1, Act 2 and Act 3. Act 1 is where you introduce the problem that the movie or the web series is likely to solve. Act 2 is where you build the tension and Act 3 is where the problem is resolved. Let us go through these acts in a bit more detail.

Act 1 constitutes about 25 per cent of the movie or the web series in terms of time. If you exceed that time in introducing the problem, you are taking too long to get to 'the hook' to hold on to an audience.

What are common types of problems that are generally seen?

Boy meets girl. Boy likes girl. Girl is out of boy's league. Most romantic movies follow this problem statement.

The hero/heroine comes from a humble background. He/she is trying to fight all odds to come up in life and realize his/

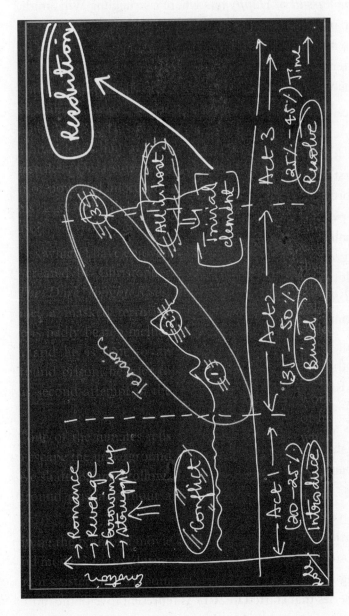

Figure 3.1: An Overview of the Most Common Movie Structure

her dreams. This is a classic struggle story. Think of movies like *The Pursuit of Happyness* where a struggling Will Smith, with no place to stay, has to take care of his son. He decides to take up an unpaid internship at a prestigious brokerage firm and after numerous struggles eventually goes on to become very successful in life.

Or, a certain boy from a small town in India who aspires to play cricket. No one from his part of the world has ever played for India. He doesn't have the contacts to give him that first break. He doesn't have a conventional technique to impress the selectors. He doesn't have the garrulous urban personality required to make a good first impression. Eventually, Mahendra Singh Dhoni goes on to become one of the greatest cricketers the world has ever seen by fighting the colossal odds against him. The movie *M.S. Dhoni: The Untold Story* is a story of success of the protagonist after surmounting inhuman odds.

An idiot killed John Wick's dog and now everyone must die. This is the underlying story of *John Wick*, played by superstar Keanu Reeves. This is a classical revenge story as a thug kills John Wick's dog, a dog that was gifted by his dying wife to him, as someone to love and his last beacon of hope. After this mishap, the legendary assassin John Wick comes out of retirement to craft one of the greatest franchises in revenge dramas.

Three young women join one of the most glamorous publications *Scarlet* in New York City. The series chronicles their journeys of growing up and the trials and tribulations of being a millennial in a modern-day world. *The Bold Type*, a web series that started in 2017 is representative of the more nuanced 'coming of age' problem statement.

The problem statement is critical as it sets the tone for the rest of the movie or the web series. The rest of the movie or the web series is essentially going to be a resolution for this statement.

Some of you may ask what happens if the problem statement is weak?

Well, a question is often asked, why the last few movies of a certain Indian superstar are bombing at the box office. The answer is very simple, poor or delayed problem statement definition.

Can you think of other types of problem statements? What do you think the problem statement of the *Fast and the Furious* franchise is?

Act 2 is essentially where the conflict or the problem statement is amplified and the tension is built. The key question is how much tension should be built. If you don't have adequate tension, then you are not satisfied as it was not enough of a struggle. If you have TOO much tension, then you might think this is too boring and unnecessarily dragging. For instance, if the guy gets the girl to say yes in the first attempt, you might go 'blah'. Similarly, your head might explode if the guy struggles to get the girl after 8 attempts. That is borderline stalking and totally creepy.

The right amount of struggle is actually derived from a storytelling principle in Chapter 2 titled 'How Does Your Brain React to Storytelling?', the Rule of 3. Your brain forms a pattern in the third instance. Less than 3, it can't. More than 3, it is too much effort. Hence, movie writers often show a struggle twice after which everything seems lost. After everything seems lost, a trivial element is introduced which helps the lead make a comeback and often succeed in the third attempt.

Sounds too complicated? Let's take a few examples.

In the series *House* which chronicles the journey of a brilliant but temperamental doctor Gregory House, this principle is explored in great detail. In every episode, Gregory House's treatments often go wrong during the first and second attempts, almost leaving the patient on the verge of disaster. The trivial element that always rescues him is a water cooler conversation with his good friend James Wilson. This water cooler exchange, the trivial element, often leads him to save the patient's life, just before disaster strikes. On a side note, *House* also has a fantastic collection of powerful anecdotes. How did Gregory House injure his leg? Why did Stacy Warner, his old girlfriend, leave House?

Moving on, one of the movie franchises which I have enjoyed the most is the *Batman* franchise created by Christopher Nolan. In the 2012 blockbuster, *The Dark Knight Rises*, Batman emerges back to fight Bane, a masked terrorist. In his first interaction with Bane, he is badly beaten including a crippling blow to his back, and he is sent to an underground prison. In the underground prison, he tries to escape but fails to do so. This is his second attempt in the struggle.

The trivial element at play is when one of the inmates tells Batman that a child had managed to escape the underground prison without the help of a protective shaft. Batman follows that advice and escapes the underground prison without a protective shaft.

The role of the trivial element in defining the path of a movie is legendary. In the superhit Bollywood movie *3 Idiots*, during the climax scene where Kareena Kapoor's sister enters labour during pregnancy and there is unexpected flooding and power outages, Aamir Khan uses a power source termed 'Virus' he created as a non-consequential project during the first half of the movie to save her.

In the 1975 blockbuster movie *Deewar* that catapulted Amitabh Bachchan to megastardom in India, Amitabh Bachchan wore a plate with the letters '786', considered to be lucky and a chant to the holy God. In the climax of the movie, the trivial element is indicated by this plate slipping out of Amitabh Bachchan's arm, indicating an ominous turn of events ahead. Amitabh Bachchan, the anti-establishment hero, is shot dead by his own brother, the policeman Shashi Kapoor.

Act 2 is often characterized by great negative performances. A negative lead helps immensely in building up the tension in Act 2. Think of Joker. Think of Bane. Think of the Shark in *Jaws*. Think of the dinosaur in *Jurassic Park*. Think of life in general in *The Pursuit of Happyness*.

Act 3 is where everything comes together, and it is the resolution of the problem statement and the tension that is built.

How does this resolution happen?

Boy, typically, gets girl.

John Wick manages to kill his arch enemy.

Batman saves Gotham.

Dr Gregory House saves his patient.

Aamir Khan is recognized as an extraordinary student in *3 Idiots*.

M. S. Dhoni wins the 2011 cricket world cup.

Will Smith makes an extraordinary career in *The Pursuit of Happyness*.

However, Act 3 is far more nuanced, and it is not just about a simple resolution. Act 3 and the ending are characterized by a unique twist at the end. And the twist is often the defining part of the movie.

In the 1999 blockbuster movie, *The Sixth Sense*, a young child is haunted by his ability to see ghosts. He is visited by a child psychologist, Bruce Willis, to help him recover from this disturbing ability. After realizing his supernatural abilities, Bruce Willis encourages the young boy to help the ghosts he sees and to aid them to finish their business. The young boy helps many ghosts trying to find closure at the end. The twist in the movie is that the child psychologist, Bruce Willis, is actually a ghost who has been dead throughout the entire movie, and the young boy is helping him find closure.

In the 1960 legendary movie, *Psycho*, a hotel owner, Norman Bates finds the women he is interested in supposedly getting stabbed by his mother because of envy and jealousy. After each person goes missing, one of the family members lands up at the hotel in search of the missing member, but they also get stabbed. The twist, and it's one of the most famous ones in cinematic history, is that Norman had murdered his mother a decade back and kept her body as a mummy. He created an alternate personality in his mind, his mother, jealous and possessive of him as he felt towards his mother. He committed all the murders once his 'mother' personality took over.

What are some other movies and web series with great twists at the end?

The Usual Suspects.

Seven.

How to Get Away with Murder?

Game of Thrones.

The Prestige.

Shutter Island.

Why is the twist considered so important? If you recall from the previous chapter, your brain treats the ending as a major element in defining the overall experience. Such pioneering research identified the importance of the ending about a couple of decades ago. Fortunately, movie script writers knew about the importance of the ending about a century ago. Hence, so much importance is given to the ending.

Once a movie or a web series has been created, the most important principle that is deployed is the principle of minimalism or cutting out the unnecessary flab. Every 5-second film is deleted and then checked whether the movie stands on its own. If it does, it is treated as flab and ruthlessly trimmed. The end product of such an exercise is a super tight script that your brain likes. Your brain loves minimalistic fast-paced scripts because it has a short attention span and wants to get to the point fast.

This is why some of you LOVE my videos on YouTube. Now I am sure you are curious and bound to check out my channel. Please do.

There are more nuances to the art of writing a movie script. The movie can be narrated backward in time (e.g., *Memento*) or the ending can be shown first (e.g., *Fight Club* or *The Hangover*) or structures can be non-linear (e.g., *Pulp Fiction*).

Fortunately for you, this book is written in a linear style with no liberties taken. Or is it?

You will find something very interesting when you come to the last chapter of this book. By the way, if you are going to be smart and read the last chapter of this book after the current chapter, you aren't going to get the twist.

METAPHORS, SYMBOLS AND COLOURS

While filming a movie, the role of metaphors, symbols and colours is massive. Sometimes they become central to storytelling. As we will find out in the next few paragraphs.

In the movie *Inception*, Leonardo DiCaprio always carries a spinning top with him. If the top keeps spinning, it means he is in a dreamworld. If the top stops spinning, it means he is entering reality. Interestingly, in the last scene of the movie, when Leonardo DiCaprio comes back to his family and spins his top to see if he is in a dream world or in reality, the movie ends on an open note and we don't know whether the top keeps spinning or it stops.

Similarly, in the Oscar-winning movie, *Parasite*, the 'rock' plays a pivotal role in the movie. In the movie, the Kim family, impoverished, is gifted a rock as it is supposed to bring prosperity. The rock shows its power, and one by one, members of the Kim family start working for one of the well-to-do families, the Parks. The rock, metaphorically implying social mobility and moving up in life, turns out to be a fake one at the end of the movie. The movie has a tragic ending with the Park family patriarch getting killed by the father of the Kim family, and the latter going into hiding in the basement of that house.

In the 2019 blockbuster movie, *Joker*, the clown make-up has explicit meaning throughout the movie. Initially, the make-up resembles an aid for entertainment by Joker. It goes on to represent the different societies the regular people live in Gotham. And eventually, it becomes a sign of rebellion against the ruling elite. Along similar lines, think of the movie, *V for Vendetta*, where the mask plays a critical role in the movie.

Colour and lighting play an incredibly important role too. In a TED talk given by Danielle Feinberg, Director of Photography at Pixar Animation Studios, she speaks about the incredible role lighting and colour play in changing the entire experience of a movie. She speaks of the role of lighting to bring the underwater stories to life in *Finding Nemo*. In the talk and in a subsequent interview, she speaks about how lighting and colour are the backbones of emotion. In an interview about the 2008 robot movie, *WALL-E*, she says,

> We had to do massive visual storytelling because there's no dialogue—only robot beeps. Yet, we needed the audience to understand that we're on Earth, that it's polluted and that WALL-E's the last one left. So we limited the colour palette to tans and oranges. Our production designer was adamant that there be no green anywhere, because he wanted a visual punch when WALL-E finds a plant for the first time. Your eyes have been washed in a limited colour palette and suddenly there's intense green. It cerebrally makes a difference.[1]

PRINCIPLES OF STORYTELLING

Take a few seconds and write down alongside a sheet of paper, what are the principles of storytelling that the world of movies and web series hint at?

---

[1] The link to the interview where she provides fascinating insights on how Pixar Animation Studios uses colour and lighting in their blockbuster movies: https://ideas.ted.com/how-color-helps-a-movie-tell-its-story/

The easiest one to spot is the need for a clear problem definition. A movie or a web series without a clear conflict to resolve is headed for disaster. This simple insight is one of the major problems why so many transformation journeys fail in large companies. This is one of the reasons why so many fancy consulting assignments fail in large organizations.

How do you communicate by leveraging the principles from the world of movies? The three- act structure is an old one that is taught to debaters the world over. The number 3 is magical because less than 3, your brain cannot form a pattern. More than 3, it takes more effort to form a pattern.

While speaking, the 'Rule of 3' manifests as follows: set up the problem, tell them about the challenges and speak to them about the resolution.

When you speak to CEOs, you talk in 'Sets of 3'—3 key steps, 3 key actions, 3 key pain points.

Your brain appreciates the ending in an experience, and it measures the whole experience by the quality of the ending. This has numerous applications in business and in defining corporate turnarounds, consumer shopping experiences, rock concerts, change management, and so on.

Minimalism has applications in your personal and corporate life. We will see how minimalism is leveraged in the world of business through corporate presentations and to a certain extent in how it drives your business productivity.

Powerful anecdotes hold onto your attention like nothing else because of chemicals realized in your brain. When you see Will Smith struggling to get a meal for his son in *The Pursuit of Happyness*, your brain generates oxytocin, the empathy chemical. When communicating to a large audience, tactically releasing chemicals in your audience's brain through powerful anecdotes is very handy.

Never underestimate the power of symbols, metaphors and colours. In a later chapter, we will discuss an interesting branch of science called semiotics and how you can use that to make your communication stick.

We will explore all of these in subsequent chapters in Parts 2 and 3 of this book.

Before we move on to the next set of chapters, I want to crystallize the major principles of storytelling that I have touched upon till now.

THE 10 GOLDEN RULES OF STORYTELLING

1. Storytelling is the main reason we as a species are alive today. It will be the #1 reason your corporation or start-up will be alive tomorrow. It is the single biggest skill set you will need. It will impact every aspect of your life, personal and professional.

2. Storytelling is gripping because it releases certain chemicals in your brain. By knowing how to tactfully release those chemicals in your audience's brain, you can get people hooked on your message.

3. Your brain judges an experience primarily by its ending rather than how long it takes or what happens in the middle. This finding is profound and has applications in several areas.

4. Your brain loves communication in 'groups of 3'. Less than 3, it can't form a pattern. More than 3, it becomes effort intensive for your brain.

5. Your brain loves minimalistic communication as it is fundamentally lazy and has an entire body to run. Cut off all the flab.

6. Your brain loves a powerful anecdote. It loves to visualize itself in that anecdote. It always chooses an

anecdote over a number. A Nested Anecdote becomes incredibly powerful.

7. Your brain loves a story provided the problem statement is clear. If the problem statement isn't clear, your brain treats the experience like a snooze fest.

8. Your brain loves popular culture references. It immediately connects with what is commonly available to everyone. It just gets it. Also, never underestimate the power of symbols, metaphors and colour. It is often central to storytelling.

9. While narrating a story, your brain loves the tension, the build-up or the challenges. In simple English, the 'why' is supremely important.

10. And most importantly, reread these 9 principles mentioned above. The rest of the book will show you how these get applied across a variety of situations.

The future is shaped by your dreams,
so stop wasting time and go to sleep.

Anonymous, on the internet

Folks, I don't trust children.
They're here to replace us.

Stephen Colbert, American comedian

CHAPTER 4

OUR WORLD IN THE NEXT FEW YEARS

Welcome to the fourth chapter of this book!

Let us take a pause for a second and understand what has been covered till now. In one sentence, we have studied the past or our history.

In Chapter 1, we looked at why storytelling is the primary reason you are alive and reading this book.

In Chapter 2, we looked at the world of behavioural psychology and neuroscience to understand the principles of storytelling that impact your brain.

In Chapter 3, we looked at the glamorous world of movies to identify principles of storytelling that have been used historically.

The common thread, with all three chapters till now, is that they explore the past. We are trying to learn from our past. However, while it is important to understand the past, you are reading this book to succeed in the future. So in this chapter, we will look at 'five big futures' that are likely to become prominent in our lives over the next few years and how storytelling is going to help you succeed as those futures take central shape in our lives.

Fasten your seat belts and enjoy the world view of the future.

To be honest, all five futures are happening in some form right now, but they will scale up significantly over the next five to eight years.

FUTURE #1: THE GLOBALIZATION OF POP CULTURE

Ironically, as we look to understand our future, we will look at our past again. The reason why storytelling is the primary tool that you are alive today is that it can get millions of people under one roof to share a common set of ideals.

Over the past hundreds of years, religion and political systems have been the two big storytelling hooks. Over the last 200 years, it has been the notion of a corporate, football club or a movie franchise. The future symbols that will bring people under one roof are likely to be pop culture.

My first touch point with South Korean culture was when I reluctantly decided to give in to peer pressure and watch the first episode of *Squid Games*. This was when it was Netflix's top show across 80 countries and *Squid Games* mania was taking over the world. If you haven't seen the show, it is a South Korean drama series in which hundreds, 456 to be precise, of cash-strapped people are invited to participate in a game show where each round is a children's game with a huge cash bounty at the end. The only catch is that if you fail to win a game, you are killed. Yes, killed! Only one person survives till the end and over 400 participants die along the way.

I found the premise disgusting and perverted. I saw the first episode and binge-watched the nine episodes of Season 1 at one go. Despite the grotesque construct, some of the values of class inequality, high rentals to stay in an apartment, massive debt, income disparity, a rigged system, the corrupt bankers resonated with people the world over and brought millions of people under one roof to watch this deadly, pun totally intended, drama.

The popularity of *Squid Games* led to numerous commercial ventures like the rise of retro tracksuits that the participants and the guards wear through the movie. There are restaurants and theme parks across many cities in the world that are designed around the concept of 'Squid Games'. You will have access to the next course of a seven-course meal if you finish the game in each course. Obviously, you are not killed if you don't finish the game at the end of each course!

So is the interest in Dalgona candy. Dalgona candy is a Korean dessert made of melted sugar and baking soda. In a particular episode of *Squid Games*, you are supposed to cut out a triangle, square, circle or umbrella without breaking the candy. Try this, if you haven't done it yet. It is not easy. Especially, when your life is at stake.

The rise of pop culture soft power from East Asia, South Korea and Japan is not an isolated one. While I don't scream like teenagers listening to the boy and girl bands from South Korea, for instance, BTS or Bangtan Boys, their influence in exercising soft power is unmistakable.

Some of the themes that *Squid Games* explored have also been explored in the Oscar-winning movie *Parasite*. In the movie, a struggling family sees an opportunity to work with a rich family and soon all of them find a way to live in that household and lead a parasitic life on the rich family. Or, as the movie hints towards the end, is it the rich family leading a parasitic life on the poor family?

The rise of global bestselling dramas is not restricted to these two series. There is also *Sweet Home* and *Alice in Borderland*.

In the Korean series, *Sweet Home*, released at the end of 2020 on Netflix, the gripping horror drama revolves around humans turning into savage monsters as they are infected, and one troubled teenager and his neighbours have to fight them as everyone around them turns into monsters. This home is anything but sweet.

In the Japanese series, *Alice in Borderland*, again released towards the end of 2020 on Netflix, an obsessed gamer 'Arisu' suddenly finds himself in an emptied version of Tokyo in which he and his friends must compete in dangerous games in order to survive. The series was in the Top 10 shows in more than 50 countries around the world. I recommend you to watch this show in case you haven't.

Such a rise in global storytelling is not restricted to eastern Asia. *Fauda* is an Israeli television series drawing on the protagonist's experiences in the Israeli Defence Forces as they pursue a Hamas terrorist known as 'The Panther'.

Lupin, a French mystery thriller, is about the protagonist 'Assane Diop', a man who is inspired by the adventures of the master thief 'Arsene Lupin'. The series portrays Assane's journey in plotting revenge for his father's death. The series was watched by over 70 million households during its first month, making it one of the biggest non-English series on Netflix, including a #1 slot in countries as varied as Brazil, Vietnam, Germany, Philippines and Sweden.[1]

The single biggest theme that is coming out of the above narrative is the globalization of storytelling. Over the next decade, great stories are as likely to come out of Los Angeles

---

[1] I loved Lupin. Interesting statistics on the show: Manori Ravindran, 'Lupin' Will Be Seen By 70 Million Subscribers, Netflix Claims,' *Variety*, https://variety.com/2021/tv/global/lupin-netflix-omar-sy-70-million-viewers-1234887688/

as they are out of South Korea, Vietnam, Israel, Argentina and Senegal. In this case, globalization is actually going to be a good thing as these series are going to represent their local cultures accurately and bring about a great appreciation of the struggles these cultures have gone through.

As pop culture references are a critical element in crafting master storytelling, pop culture references are likely to evolve consistently over the next few years.

Not just the stereotypes of Hollywood but far more nuanced and globally representative ones also.

In a future storytelling narrative, if you have to showcase a shrewd protagonist, instead of showing James Bond, you might choose to show Assane Diop.

FUTURE #2: DIGITIZATION POST THE PANDEMIC

I don't need to tell you how your work has changed after the pandemic. You would have been working from home for the most part of 2020, 2021 and some part of 2022 also. As you read this book, you may have moved to a hybrid working structure of working 3 days in the office and 2 days from home.

A study by McKinsey, 'Future of Work after coronavirus disease 2019 (COVID-19)', quotes that 20–25 per cent of workers in advanced countries could work remotely 3 days and above every week on a long-term basis while 15–20 per cent of workers could work remotely 1–2 days a week on a long- term basis.

This might be slightly lesser in emerging countries as agriculture is a significant source of employment. In case you are wondering why you can't do remote work in agriculture, you can't sow paddy seeds through a Zoom call. Also, certain Asian cultures are notorious for making employees sit

12 hours a day 6 days a week. Have you heard of the term 996 in China? Some companies are notorious, not just in China but in many other Asian countries, for making employees work 9 AM to 9 PM 6 days a week.

Whichever part of the world you may be in, hybrid working is here to stay. During the pandemic, Zoom saw a 300 per cent increase in its user base during the pandemic.[2] And this is going to be our reality.

How does this impact you from a storytelling perspective? Well, storytelling is much easier when it is face to face. It is much tougher on a call when 80 per cent of the screen is focused on your slide and your face is hidden in a corner. However, you need not worry. In Chapters 9 and 10 titled 'Creating Brilliant Presentations' and 'Making Elements Stick' of this book, respectively, we will look at how you can master written storytelling and how you can use it to navigate very tricky situations like having to tell someone, 'Mate, you really suck'.

This increase in digitization is not restricted to the way we work. There is going to be a huge uptick in enterprise technology infrastructure. Enterprise infrastructure like cloud computing, where you put all your IT infrastructure on a cloud hosted by a technology giant and you pay only for what you consume, is likely to grow by 25 per cent at least for the next five to seven years.[3]

Similarly, the use of enterprise software to drive productivity in sales, marketing, service and collaboration is going to see

---

[2] A very interesting article from Forbes on the software trends in the post pandemic world: Manish Mittal, 'Software Trends in the Post-Pandemic World,' *Forbes*, https://www.forbes.com/sites/forbestechcouncil/2021/09/08/software-trends-in-the-post-pandemic-world/?sh=1fedc2a422dc

[3] Given you love footnotes so much, read this! Fortune Business Insights, *Key Market Insights*, https://www.fortunebusinessinsights.com/cloud-storage-market-102773

a phenomenal rise over the next few years. The same article I referred to earlier suggests that such productivity software has grown over 50 per cent in the year 2020 alone.

What does all this mean for you as an aspirational master storyteller? If you are in the field of technology, you have a bright future and storytelling can make you a brilliant salesperson. In Chapter 8 titled 'Driving Corporate B2B Sales' of this book, we look at how you can use principles of storytelling to buy your dream BMW from your massive bonus.

Also, large companies will be undertaking massive digital transformation programmes and you will be leading a lot of them. This shift towards large transformation programmes is due to consumers moving online for shopping or expecting a technology-enhanced experience in the physical retail store. Historically, more than half of such programmes have been duds and failures. In Chapter 5 titled 'Driving Change' of this book, we will look at how you can use principles of storytelling to master the transformation journeys for these companies.

FUTURE #3: EVERYONE IS GOING TO BE AN INFLUENCER

To be honest, I was fairly pessimistic about live streaming before the pandemic.

Why would you want to watch some 20-year-old apply lipstick, eat noodles or unbox the latest iPhone in front of you? Probably, I get it once in a while but to be crazily devoted to it was beyond my imagination.

However, like the many mysteries of the world, live streaming and commerce through influencers have taken off through the roof. According to a Forbes estimate, over 500 million people in China would have watched live streams in 2020 alone and this number is likely to grow disproportionately.[4] Not just that, commerce through live streams is expected to go through the roof too.

Before we go into how big it is likely to become, a basic question is why is this happening?

The answer is very simple. Trust is eroding in traditional institutions. For instance, about 15 per cent of Americans refused to get vaccinated despite the havoc the pandemic has created. Some just didn't trust the government and the vaccine.[5]

When a celebrity pitches a soft drink loaded with sugar and calories to you but speaks of her healthy lifestyle on Instagram, she smells of hypocrisy.

The Edelman Trust Barometer which measures public trust in institutions claims that trust in technology companies is eroding and trust in technology has reached all-time lows in 17 out of 27 markets.[6] The report also says that the trust index has declined in the government in the world's two largest economies—US and China.

So you don't trust the government. You don't trust technology firms. You don't trust celebrities. Whom do you trust?

Enter the influencer. She seems a normal person like you. She doesn't seem to reek of hypocrisy. She talks your language.

---

[4] Fascinating article on the rise of live streaming in China: Michelle Greenwald, 'Live Streaming E-Commerce is the Rage in China. Is the U.S. Next?' *Forbes* https://www.forbes.com/sites/michellegreenwald/2020/12/10/live-streaming-e-commerce-is-the-rage-in-china-is-the-us-next/?sh=2681c5436535

[5] I have decided not to make any cheeky comments on the government. So just read the footnote—Lindsay M. Monte, *Household Pulse Survey Shows Many Don't Trust COVID Vaccine, Worry About Side Effects*, United States Census Bureau, https://www.census.gov/library/stories/2021/12/who-are-the-adults-not-vaccinated-against-covid.html

[6] Trust in institutions like government and technology firms is declining: Richard Edelman, '2021 Edelman Trust Barometer Trust in Technology,' Edelman, https://www.edelman.com/trust/2021-trust-barometer/trust-technology

She understands you. She doesn't endorse brands that you may not like. All of this is available within one click on Instagram, TikTok, Alibaba, Taobao Live, etc.

Going forward, everyone is going to be an influencer, including, you and me. Why do you think I am writing this? You need to influence your future employer about your capabilities. You need to influence your peers about your stature. You need to influence your boss about what you are capable of. You may want to disseminate information to your community to come across as an expert to help your career.

I am sure I don't need to remind you how competitive the world has become. Social media is an extremely powerful vehicle to establish this for you.

In India, YouTube says there are more than 40,000 channels with over 100,000 subscribers. My channel is getting close to the magical 100,000 mark. In case you haven't subscribed to my channel till now, you should do it and get me closer to the 100,000 mark! Coming back, over 2 million people have registered for the YouTube Partner Program through which they qualify to earn money from ad revenue. Grow this by 25 per cent over the next five years and you see where this is headed.[7]

In Chapter 14 titled 'Creating Your Personal Brand', we will go through a journey in terms of how you can become an effective influencer using the principles of storytelling.

There is also a corporate angle to this. As we will see in a future chapter, the single biggest marketing theme in the future might be converting a product into an experience.

---

[7] Do you want to become a successful YouTuber? Your future might be bright. Vishal Mathur, 'YouTube India's Creator Impact: 2 mn-strong Community, Revenue Streams, et al.' *Hindustan Times*. https://www.hindustantimes.com/business/youtube-india-s-creator-impact-2-mn-strong-community-revenue-streams-et-al-101646304789091.html

Now, when you eat a packet of chips, you buy the packet, rip it open, stuff the chips into your mouth and throw the packet. As simple as that. This is how I and my friends eat it. We love deep-fried sliced potatoes with loads of salt.

More and more brands are turning this hogging of chips into a memorable experience. When you go to a store, there will be a nice song that will be played to calm you down. If you want to put your headphones on, you can hear music that will make you appreciate the texture of the potato by appealing to your senses. By logging into a YouTube channel, you will get free recipes of how this packet of chips can be used to make 10 other delicious recipes. You will also be told about exercises which you can try to burn the calories you get by eating the chips. By scanning the QR code on the packet, you can appreciate where the potato was sourced from and if the potato farmers are being treated well in that whole chain.

As most brands turn their products into experiences, you will notice the huge role that content and sensory experiences are playing in this transformation.

Going forward, every brand will be a content company.

Going forward, every brand will sell an experience.

In Chapter 7 titled 'Creating Legendary Consumer Brands', we will look at how storytelling will drive this transformation for you as brands endorse content and experiences.

FUTURE #4: EVERYTHING META, WEB 3.0, CRYPTO AND INTERNET OF SENSES

In case you are not sure what the above line means and if you think it is from the world of quantum physics, you need to worry. Just read patiently through the following paragraphs.

The metaverse, or the virtual platform that mirrors the real world is already going live in a few applications. In a piece for Forbes that I wrote on the metaverse, I highlighted how multiplayer gaming, employee onboarding and the world of dating are already on the metaverse.[8] Think of a multiplayer gaming environment where a gamer is interacting with her peer players, live streaming her entire game and strategy with her thousands of devout followers, has merchandising on the gaming platform, say her branded line of T-shirts that you can buy using crypto, and generates a token, the first time she crossed Level 7 in the game, which you can buy and resell but the ownership will always say that it belonged to her initially and all the logs will be clear. This is the metaverse.

Or think of Novak Djokovic and Rafael Nadal battling it out on Roland Garros, the French Open, with both tied on 24 grand slams and one of them trying to be the undisputed 'Greatest of All Time'. While it is difficult to get a ticket for this prestigious match in real life, but in the metaverse, with your virtual reality (VR) sets, you can pretend to sit in the best seat in the house and watch the two tennis legends battle it out in REAL time.

Or, interestingly, you can take your date out in the metaverse on the surface of Mars. In case this sounds preposterous to you, there are start-ups today which can facilitate a date in the metaverse on the surface of the moon. Given Elon Musk's obsession with Mars, I am sure that day is not far away.

How will storytelling change in such a scenario?

While the basic principles of real-world storytelling will remain the same in the virtual world, however, due to enhanced

---

[8] In case you want to read the whole piece on where the metaverse is headed: Sandeep Das, 'Oh Metaverse, My Metaverse: A Simpleton's Guide to Understanding the New Buzzword,' *Forbes*, https://www.forbesindia.com/blog/technology/oh-metaverse-my-metaverse-a-simpletons-guide-to-understanding-the-new-buzzword/

technology, the ability to interact with your consumer will multiply manifold.

In Chapter 7 titled 'Creating Legendary Consumer Brands', we will look at how the element of interactivity is playing out in brand storytelling.

Also, there has been an ever-increasing rise in digital media consumption. In many countries, the spending on digital media is now eclipsing the spending on traditional media like TV and radio.

WEB 3.0

Web 3.0 is an interesting premise. Web 1.0 is the internet of the 1990s where you had static web pages and you could scroll and consume information.

Web 2.0 is the current version of the internet where you can consume information, watch videos, interact with your peers on social media and create content as an influencer on a platform like YouTube or Instagram. This is due to the rise of powerful smartphones and cheap internet which has given rise to the gig economy.

However, there are certain concerns with Web 2.0 which might not be there in Web 3.0. In Web 2.0, power is in the hands of a few large technology companies, such as Facebook, Google. Also, some of these algorithms are locked and kept secure, away from the knowledge of the common layperson. And no one really knows the exact log of transactions.

Web 3.0 as a concept is interesting. The entire construct of the internet will move from a centralized source, in the hands of a few technology companies, to a decentralized model owned by the end users. There is transparency as transactions will be conducted over blockchain and hence the logs will be visible and secure. The power will increase as more and more devices in your home, like fridges and TVs, get connected to Web 3.0.

Needless to say, there are risks. Without content moderation, this is likely to produce a toxic online environment with bullying and harassment.

If you are a content influencer, you don't have to go through a platform like YouTube. You can engage with your community directly and not go through a centralized platform. Similarly, if you are a brand trying to engage with your loyal community of followers.

In Chapter 14 titled 'Creating Your Personal Brand', we will touch upon the principles of storytelling you can use to tap into this booming Web 3.0.

INTERNET OF SENSES

Internet of Senses, in my view, is the big disruptor in the making. Internet of Senses involves using all the senses—touch, sound, sight and smell enabled by digital technologies to enhance the consumer experience.

Let me give you an example.

There is a cafe in Shanghai 'Xin Cafe' that launched a 'Sonic Sweetener' cup in 2017. Whenever you take a sip from this cup, a high-pitched musical sound is emitted via an attached headphone. Three out of five visitors felt that their coffee tasted sweeter when they heard this noise. For the health-conscious consumer trying to limit consumption of sugar, this is a huge development.[9]

---

[9] Isn't this experiment fascinating? Asia Ad Junkie, 'Sonic Sweetener? Interesting Campaign in Chinese Cafe to Reduce Sugar Consumption,' London International Awards, https://www.brandinginasia.com/dentsu-sonic-sweetener-china/

I think this is a very interesting way to reduce sugar consumption. I wish they had a way to reduce my love for oily food. Maybe, I can eat carrots and the Internet of Senses will convince my brain that I am eating a greasy burger. If they make such an invention, they should be given the Nobel Prize.

In Chapter 7 titled 'Creating Legendary Consumer Brands', we will look at how the Internet of Senses is being used by brands as part of their storytelling experience to convey the product as an experience story.

FUTURE #5: THE ENTREPRENEURIAL DREAM

Let me start this theme with an anecdote.

Five years ago, in India, if you told your neighbour that you were an entrepreneur, your neighbour would have sympathized with you that you do not have a job. There is no way ever you could have dated their son or daughter. Even if you were perfect 'dating material'.

Now, if you go to the same neighbour and quote your start-up's valuations and if it has a nice collection of animal names like 'unicorn' attached to it, your neighbour will ensure that his son or daughter turns up to have dinner with you at a nice place. He might pick up the check too.

Now, let me throw some numbers at you. As I write this chapter, there are 1,000 unicorns or companies which have valuations in excess of 1 billion dollars across the world.[10] By the time you read this chapter, the number would most likely have doubled or increased by 50 per cent.

Why has this happened?

---

[10] Do you want to know the list of Unicorn companies the world over? Some of you will be on this list someday. Be my guest and read—CBInsights, 'The Complete List of Unicorn Companies,' https://www.cbinsights.com/research-unicorn-companies

The rise of smartphones? Definitely.

Super cheap internet the world over? A big yes.

Super easy private equity capital? Maybe the main reason.

Over the last decade, capital to invest in start-up firms could be procured at near-zero interest rates. Also, there was a cultural change in societies with young entrepreneurs in their 20s and 30s turning into millionaires if not billionaires overnight.

However, not all of this story is hunky-dory. A lot of start-ups keep burning cash and they will never be profitable. Some premium firms, like Tesla or Facebook, will burn cash for a few years and then turn supremely profitable.

During that period of uncertainty, in the first few years, the entrepreneur has to go around managing stakeholders—investors, employees and most importantly consumers. In proverbial language, the entrepreneur, he or she, has to sell a story!

And it is that one quality that will help him or her bring everyone together under one roof.

In Chapter 6 titled 'Becoming a Visionary Entrepreneur', we will explore how you can leverage storytelling to take your neighbour's attractive son or daughter for a date. Everything paid for by your neighbour.

It should be very obvious to you that the entrepreneurial dream is going to accelerate over the next few years.

In the emerging world, bringing the unorganized market comprising of retailers and consumers to the organized space is a huge opportunity. So is the space around health and wellness. Not to forget education.

In the B2B space, anything to do with technology—cloud computing, software as a service or cyber security is going to be supremely attractive.

To be honest, there are many more futures that are possible. Some of them are as follows:

The unpleasant rise of depression.

Global conflict.

Wealth inequality.

Class inequality.

Living life on your terms.

The rise of spirituality and psychedelics.

The focus on sustainability.

But in this chapter, I have highlighted the five (Figure 4.1) where I see the maximum impact of storytelling.

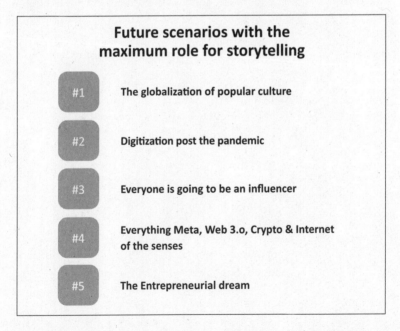

Figure 4.1: Five Future Scenarios That Have the Maximum Impact of Storytelling

PART 2

STORYTELLING FOR CORPORATES

How can you use storytelling to drive transformation or change in a large corporate?

How can you leverage storytelling as an entrepreneur?

How can you use storytelling to create legendary brands in the future?

How can you use storytelling to drive B2B sales or in consulting?

I welcome change as long as nothing is altered or different than before.

Anonymous on the internet

Men marry women with the hope they will never change. Women marry men with the hope they will change. Invariably, they are both disappointed.

Albert Einstein, I am sure you know who he is

CHAPTER 5

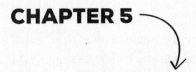

DRIVING CHANGE

The single biggest word you will hear in your professional career is not the 'pandemic', not 'entrepreneurship', not becoming a 'millionaire' but 'transformation'. Transformation implies changing your company and making it 'future ready' due to digitization or due to the changing world or adopting a new business model.

In case you are not convinced, consider the following.

Once upon a time, the President of the United States used this phone. At its peak, it had 80 million users worldwide, including me. Today it is barely present.

What happened to Blackberry?

In 1975, they created the first digital camera but were concerned that it might cannibalize their photographic film business. This company, a giant in the world of cameras, eventually went bankrupt in 2012 after the smartphone came with a built-in camera.

What happened to Kodak?

This provider of video game rentals had 84,000 people and 9,000 outlets at its peak. It had the opportunity to buy Netflix for 50 million dollars. Read it again—50 million and not 50 billion dollars. It filed for bankruptcy in 2010, ironically gobbled up by, you guessed it right, Netflix.

What happened to Blockbuster?

The single biggest mistake they all made is that they failed to transform their business and embrace that change. As a result, they perished. This need to transform has increasingly become more important after the pandemic and over this upcoming decade.

As e-commerce scales up, chatbots become routine, drone deliveries become commonplace, employees resign brutally, corporate IT functions move towards the cloud, mental health issues become more severe, the metaverse becomes a part of our reality, countries fight with each other more and more, crypto rises as an alternate currency and the cry for sustainable energy gets louder, you will need to transform your business and your role much faster than everyone else. Not to succeed. But just to SURVIVE.

WHY SHOULD YOU WORRY?

You will lead transformation or change management journeys irrespective of whether you are in IT, sales, finance, consulting or marketing. You will lead transformation or change management journeys irrespective of the industries you operate in. You will lead them irrespective of the country you are in. You will lead them irrespective of whether you work for a large corporate, a small corporate or you are an entrepreneur.

Leading and being part of transformation journeys will be a huge part of your corporate career. A MASSIVE PART.

To be honest, such high-profile transformation journeys can be highly lucrative. Because such programmes are highly visible to the CEO or the investors, if you do a good job, your career can grow disproportionately. Likewise, in case you don't do a good job, it can go downhill at the same rate.

Interestingly, you will notice that this transformation is going to be led by technology. For instance, a company might want to go on a transformation journey around,

How do we grow our e-commerce channel?

How do we go paperless for all our corporate functions?

How do we digitize our sales teams and their workings?

How do we move our operations to the cloud?

Out of curiosity, how many transformation journeys with technology do you think are successful? Think for a couple of seconds and arrive at a percentage.

Some of you might say 80 per cent of all technology transformation journeys are successful. The more pessimistic ones might say 50 per cent. Most people hover in the interval of 50–80 per cent.

The reality is far worse. According to a *Harvard Business Review*[1] study, 70 per cent of all transformation journeys fail. In my experience in consulting for over a decade, this number is actually higher. To be honest, this is not due to the lack of intent and commitment from the leadership or the team members. The reason is very different.

Why does this happen?

It is very simple. You and I, as humans, don't like change. We don't like a disruption in our routines. This becomes more pronounced as we get older.

Your brain is lazy. Period.

Imagine changing your email sending software from Microsoft Outlook to say, Lotus Notes at the age of 43. Ewwww. You would rather start going to the gym every day.

---

[1] Link to the article, a very interesting one indeed: Nitin Nohria and Michael Beer, 'Cracking the Code of Change,' *Harvard Business Review*, https://hbr.org/2000/05/cracking-the-code-of-change

In addition, you also start asking the following uncomfortable questions:

What is in it for me?

Why should I do it?

Why do I need to change?

What happens if we don't change?

What if the new system doesn't work?

A SIMILAR ROAD TO SUCCESS AND FAILURE

When you transform your company by implementing a new digital system or driving a new organizational structure or a new business model, the journey of change goes typically as shown in Figure 5.1. To clarify, a desired turnaround at a company like the ones Apple, Netflix, Starbucks, LEGO went through in the last two decades are all transformation journeys.

As shown in Figure 5.1, the vertical axis or y-axis represents acceptance or success of the transformation and the x-axis represents time as we move through the transformation.

As a new transformation is announced by the leadership, there is a lot of excitement as there is something new on the anvil. There is a sense of hope and optimism, and there is an initial high, excitement and optimism. Think of this phase as the first 6 months of your life after marriage.

Beyond this initial euphoria, once the new system or structure starts taking roots, there are violent protests. Sometimes, there are tiny glitches in the new system and hence people magnify the glitches. Fundamentally, human beings don't like to change, and it is their natural resistance that comes to play here. They have to put in a little more effort to learn about a new system. Your brain is lazy; it doesn't want to put in that effort.

Think of this as the part of your marriage once the candlelight dinners are over.

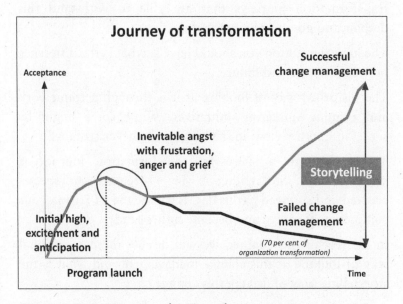

Figure 5.1: A Journey of a Transformation Programme You Will Go through Most of the Time[2]

In his talk titled, 'How to start a cultural revolution', Simon Sinek says the problem with change is that nearly two-thirds of people don't like to change because of inertia or there is concern about an uncertain future or they don't want to be the first ones driving that change.

Most transformation journeys start going downhill from here due to the negativity and the bad word of mouth from two-thirds of the population. Seventy per cent of transformation journeys fail. In my personal experience, the number is much higher.

---

[2] I have built this view with the Kubler-Ross change curve as the base.

This dip is also called the 'depth of despair' and there is numerous literature on this concept. There are only a few transformation journeys that are able to withstand this despair and go on to be successful.

The logical question you should have is what is the difference between success and failure?

The historical way of looking at it is through a framework and running numerous initiatives. While some might be successful, in my view, in the long run, it never sustains.

The answer to a successful transformation journey is STORYTELLING. Storytelling is the #1 reason our species evolved and survived to this day. It will be the #1 reason your company will evolve and become future-ready.

In the rest of this chapter, we will discuss the conventional way of looking at this change management and what is the storytelling way of driving this change.

TRADITIONAL WAY TO DRIVE CHANGE MANAGEMENT

A traditional framework to drive a successful transformation, as indicated in Figure 5.2, comprises the following.[3]

A system of REWARD is designed through incentives to nudge people—employees, vendors and consumers towards the desired behaviour as part of the transformation.

Early adopters, or about 10 per cent of the participants, are RECOGNIZED for their efforts through certificates or mementos or gifts in kind.

---

[3] There are many change management frameworks, including Prosci ADKAR model, Kurt Lewin's change model, and Satir change management model. For the nerd in you.

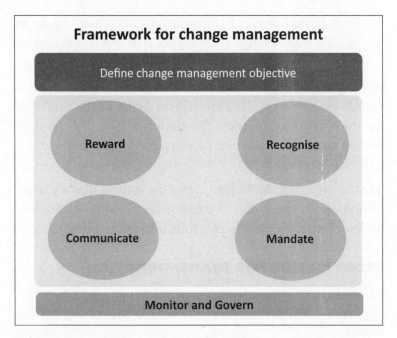

Framework for change management

Define change management objective

Reward

Recognise

Communicate

Mandate

Monitor and Govern

Figure 5.2: A Traditional Framework to Drive Effective Transformation or Change Management

There is ample COMMUNICATION through e-mails, speeches and posters by the leadership on the programme.

Worst case, there is a stick approach, a MANDATE to penalize people on their ratings or humiliate them during review sessions. Or even lay them off in case they don't seem to adapt to the new way of doing things.

Why might this approach be suboptimal?

The *Harvard Business Review* study I alluded to earlier in this chapter, interestingly points out that,

> In our experience, the reason for most of those failures is that in their rush to change their organizations, managers end up immersing themselves in an alphabet soup of initiatives.

This proliferation of recommendations often leads to muddle when change is attempted. The result is that most change efforts exert a heavy toll, both human and economic

In simple English, too many initiatives are tried without a consistent core appeal to the human being at the centre of the transformation journey. The transformation fails to carry human beings—employees, vendors and consumers under a common umbrella.

That is why historical change transformation doesn't work always. And that, ladies and gentlemen, is why storytelling will work to drive an effective transformation journey.

STORYTELLING FOR TRANSFORMATION

Before I get into these principles, some of you might have this question—How do you know these principles of storytelling work?

The answer is simple, because I have done it myself and seen it first-hand. I have also taken interest in looking at these journeys when my peers have been a part of them. And I will also tell you about a few famous global examples.

A CLEAR PROBLEM STATEMENT

Do you think that communication about a problem can go wrong? You might be surprised.

According to a Gallup poll, only 13 per cent of US employees strongly agree that their leadership communicates effectively with the organization and only 15 per cent strongly agree that their leadership makes them enthusiastic about the future.[4] In

---

[4] Scary set of numbers. Link: Vibhas Ratanjee, 'Successful Organizational Change Needs a Strong Narrative,' Workplace, https://www.gallup.com/workplace/349295/successful-organizational-change-needs-strong-narrative.aspx

simple English, most people believe that their leadership does a spectacularly poor job in communicating about the future of the organization. However, sometimes, the problem is not with communication but with the 'problem' itself.

Recall from Chapter 3 titled 'How Does Hollywood Use Storytelling', we discussed that if a movie doesn't have a clear problem statement, it becomes a torture and often bombs. I will touch upon this problem of a lack of a clear problem statement in more detail in Chapter 8 titled 'Driving Corporate B2B Sales', but I am providing you a flavour in the next few paragraphs.

A lot of business leaders interpret different things from the same statement. The following incident is a true one. For instance, if your problem statement is,

We need to be more consumer-centric as a company

Most leaders nod in unison to this statement, but they will draw different meanings in their minds. The HR head might think his consumer is the employee and you should be more employee-centric. The sales head might think the retailer is his consumer and you should be more retailer-centric. The marketing head might think the end consumer is your real consumer and you should be more end consumer-centric. The CEO might think his investors are his consumers and you should be more investor-centric.

It gets more complicated. The sales head might think you should be consumer-centric from tomorrow. The strategy head might think it will take you 3 years to get there. The marketing head might think 2 years is the right time.

The CEO might think all businesses should turn consumer-centric. The chief financial officer (CFO) might think you should target the businesses only where there is a problem because every new initiative needs money.

As an implication, whenever you are launching a transformation programme, ask yourself the metric you are tracking, the state it is in today and the state you want to take it to. More importantly, clarify the region, the channel and the time horizon.

To be consumer-centric, you may consider some of the following metrics,

Consumer loyalty

Consumer advocacy score

Net promoter index

Consumer survey index and so on.

The leadership of a company may decide that they will increase consumer loyalty score from 12 per cent to 19 per cent in 3 years' time.

More than the metric you choose, it is important that everyone speaks the same language. We will see this in more detail in Chapter 8, but I hope you get the flavour.

RULE OF 3 RULES

The human brain loves communication in groups of 3 as it is the smallest number at which the brain can form a pattern for easier recollection. Less than 3, there is no pattern, and more than 3, your brain has to put in more energy.

A lot of transformation programmes go wrong when the leadership communicates too many things, and everyone loses the core of the message. Whenever a leader communicates about the programme to a greater audience, he or she should leverage the 'Rule of 3' to answer only the following three questions,

- Why are we doing this programme?
- How will this programme help you?
- What do I need you to do in this programme?

In my experience, I have seen that some leaders are not clear on these three questions and hence the rest of the organization isn't clear. Sometimes leaders add more questions like what will we do next month, the month after that, how will we micro manage you, what targets you have to achieve, blah blah, and they make a mess of the whole communication.

A Harvard Business Review article titled 'Conversations Can Save Companies'[5] quotes the following two very interesting examples of effective storytelling to drive transformation.

In the mid-1980s, Jan Carlzon, CEO of Scandinavian Airlines Systems (SAS) was trying to turn around his business. He wanted to improve the service level of his airline and wanted to communicate effectively with his frontline workforce on what the company was trying to achieve.

They came up with a very innovative way to narrate their story. They created a booklet for their employees by using cartoon imagery like a smiling airplane to communicate why they were undertaking this transformation and how the frontline workforce was going to play a critical role. Employees eventually called this book filled with cartoon imagery the 'little red book'.

In 2008, Starbucks undertook a transformation journey to stay market competitive. Howard Schultz, the company's iconic founder, undertook a storytelling journey to carefully present the 'case for change', 'layout the plan' and 'let employees know how they can help'. Starbucks made a stunning comeback with its share price rising from around US$4 in 2008 to nearly US$120 in 2021.

---

[5] Fascinating story I think. Link to the article: Boris Groysberg and Michael Slind, 'Conversations Can Save Companies,' Harvard Business Review, https://hbr.org/2013/04/turnarounds-turn-on-conversati?registration=success

Hammering these three questions again and again in every forum plays a huge role in making a transformation pro-gramme a success and in driving stickiness in your brain.

WE LOVE POP CULTURE REFERENCES

Your brain loves popular culture. Why?

Because it is available in its recent memory and popular culture triggers the right chemicals in your brain.

I have seen the following story create magic and lift the morale of hundreds of employees in a large auditorium.

This company was on the verge of bankruptcy.

Its stocks had fallen 75 per cent in the last 4 years.

It was bleeding.

Most of its products were failing.

Its culture was toxic.

A lot of good people had left.

It was low on cash.

The product lines weren't working.

Today,

You use their phone.

You use their laptop.

You use their watch.

You use their tablet.

You use their earphones.

You use their music player.

You use their home speaker.

You use their streaming service.

In popular culture, the turnaround journey of Apple resonates very strongly with a large audience as that story is a legendary one in corporate circles. Very few stories have the ability to create the belief that if they could do it, so can we. That is the power of pop culture references.

I once saw an innovative cartoon strip around the theme of Batman. Batman, the superhero representing the transformation journey, is trying to rid Gotham of Joker, the problem being poor consumer scores. This cartoon strip is on a single page, tactically smart and often brings a smile to everyone's faces.

More importantly, it is sticky, and your journey is associated with a positive childhood memory. People love the use of popular culture references.

MAKE THE CHASE WORTH IT

Behavioural psychology has a theory called 'Scarcity Bias'. In simple English, if you visit Amazon, you might see some products with the captions '1 copy left, 2 copies left', and your brain pushes you to click the purchase button. Why does this happen?

This developed as a part of human evolution where your brain always wants you to get an important resource for you to survive. If so many people are chasing it, it must be important and good. Blame your brain for it.

How may you use this while implementing a transformation journey?

You have to make things difficult for your consumers, not easy. Read that sentence again. You have to make things difficult for the participants of your journey.

For instance, if you are launching a larger IT system for your company, you have to communicate that you are looking for 20 change agents who will be early adopters of the system.

Most companies do it till here but don't do the remaining steps. As a result, many people see this role as an additional burden. And they do it reluctantly, leading to the 70 per cent failure rate of transformation programmes.

The key is to make entering the group of 20 change agents, a matter of prestige. A matter of pure scarcity. Make your brain go totally irrational with it. How?

Set up a selection panel. Ask employees to present what value they will add. Why should you select them? Bring in their past performance into the conversation.

Get the CEO to be on the panel. Take a couple of months to select. Make them fill up three forms—paper forms.

What all of this does is, it captures your audience's attention that if something is so scarce and so much effort is being put in, it must be DAMN good.

And you will have almost everyone trying to be in the prized group of 20 early adopters.

I can vouch for this method having done this myself.

Simon Sinek, author and inspirational speaker, speaks about this exact principle in a video titled 'How to make a cultural transformation', on how he used the principle of scarcity to create demand for a transformation programme for one of his clients.[6]

POWER OF ANECDOTES

I have said it a million times till now that your brain loves powerful anecdotes over numbers any day.

How may you use this as a transformation leader?

[6] Link to the full video of his talk. The video is available on his YouTube channel: Simon Sinek, 'How to Make a Cultural Transformation,' https://www.youtube.com/watch?v=N9dONqSztWA

In case your objective is to reduce the turnaround time for complaints from eight days to four days, you will create the following testimonial,

Manish, a distributor in south Mumbai will speak in a 1-minute video on how his complaints' turnaround time has come down significantly after the transformation programme has been launched.

Such an anecdote has the power to go viral in your company and with your other distributors. However, you can claim this testimonial only if the numbers show that for at least 70 per cent of distributors, the turnaround time in complaints has reduced significantly. In case it is not applicable for the majority of people and you launch this testimonial, you may risk the perception of sounding hollow.

THE ENDING MATTERS

Recall from Chapter 2 titled 'How Does Your Brain React to Storytelling', that the way your brain works is that it remembers the ending of a journey and forgets most things along the way. Remember Mahendra Singh Dhoni hitting the winning six which is remembered as the most iconic moment of the 2011 cricket world cup.

Remember the results of that painful colonoscopy experiment.

It is important to finish your transformation journey on a high. For instance, once the distributor turnaround time for their payments or complaints has met the required target and the programme is now in a steady state, it is important to create a communication with testimonials of distributors and circulate it to the rest of the organization.

The reason this helps is because it creates a positive vibe associated with the programme and will help any subsequent transformation programme your company might undertake. People will only remember the programme by the communication you create representing the end of the programme.

As we end this chapter (refer Figure 5.3), I should tell you that I love making slides.

Some are useless.

Some are useful.

I was a consultant for a long time in my life. When I visit a temple, I write my prayer on a slide along with a beautiful image to convey my thoughts in a crystal-clear manner to God. Using the 'Rule of 3' so that God doesn't get confused in the messaging.

I am kidding.

I am surely not that crazy.

Or am I?

Figure 5.3: Impact of Storytelling on Transformation Journeys

Bad decisions make good stories.

Ellis Vidler, Author

*It could be that your purpose in life is to serve
as a warning to others.*

Ashleigh Brilliant, Author and Cartoonist

CHAPTER 6

BECOMING A VISIONARY ENTREPRENEUR

In 2009, Microsoft co-founder and philanthropist Bill Gates was invited by TED to speak on 'mosquitoes, malaria and education'. He wanted to make a point that somehow, malaria, despite its huge burden on society doesn't get the importance it should get.

Five minutes into his speech, he said the following,

'There is more money put into baldness drugs than into Malaria. Now baldness is a terrible thing and rich men are afflicted, so that's why that priority has been set. But the million deaths caused by Malaria greatly understate its impact.' He went on to add a stroke of genius storytelling next, 'Now, Malaria is transmitted by mosquitos and I have brought some here' and he released some mosquitos into the auditorium with the audience members cracking up. He ends with, 'There is no reason why only poor people should have the Malaria experience.' He finally reveals that those mosquitoes are not infected.[1] That talk, just on the TED website, has been viewed over 5 million times.

---

[1] Here is the link to the hilarious and insightful TED talk: https://www.ted.com/talks/bill_gates_mosquitos_malaria_and_education?language=en

This is brilliant storytelling at play. When Bill Gates says, there are a million deaths due to malaria every year, people understand it but don't get it. When he says, I am going to release those malaria causing mosquitoes in this auditorium, EVERYONE gets it. Including the millions who will watch the video later. The storytelling principle here is the power of the anecdote and how it is far bigger than numbers. Now Bill Gates could have run an ad campaign explaining how families suffer because of malaria but it might not have had the same impact as this speech and the innovative storytelling technique he employed.

Fast forward many years into where we are today, the amount of NOISE around us has increased disproportionately. With short-form content on the rise through TikTok and Instagram, attention spans have gone down dramatically for everyone. There are more competitors, there are more channels but only 24 hours a day for end consumers. To stand out amid all this clutter, if you are an aspiring entrepreneur and you know how to tell stories, you are way ahead of the curve. If you are an entrepreneur and if you can tell a good story, you humanize your company and can hook consumers, employees and even investors to your narrative. Powerful, isn't it? Keep reading.

DEFINE A TRANSFORMATIVE PURPOSE

In a famous interview available all over the internet, Jeff Bezos, founder of Amazon, narrates the following,

> Right after the World War 2, Morita San, the guy who founded Sony set a mission for Sony. His mission for Sony was to make Japan, not Sony, known for quality. This was a time when Japan was known for cheap copycat products. He didn't say we were going to make Sony known for quality. He said we are going to make Japan known for quality. He chose a mission for Sony that was bigger than Sony.

He goes on to explain how Amazon's purpose of being earth's most customer-centric company is a similar idea where he wants Amazon to be the benchmark for other companies when it comes to customer experience.

Any aspiring entrepreneur, if they are looking to make it REALLY big, has to craft a transformative purpose and effectively communicate that.

What is a transformative purpose? It is something that is much bigger than just market share, revenue and profitability. Why does such a transformative purpose work? It is simple, a transformative purpose is the story itself. Earlier, stories manifested as religion, political systems and nations. Now a transformative purpose, as a story, can become an incredible hook to get thousands of employees to work for you and millions of consumers to love your products. Especially, during your earlier years when your credentials are just getting established.

For instance, Tesla tries to accelerate the shift to clean energy, a purpose which is much greater than pure business numbers. SpaceX desires to sustain life through a new civilization beyond Mars. The Tata Group in India is synonymous with nation building as they try to improve the life of communities around them.[2]

However, it is important to talk the talk and walk the walk. If you, as an entrepreneur, want to improve the lives of human beings across the value chain but you source material from vendors that employ child labour, now that reeks of hypocrisy. Similarly, as an entrepreneur, if you fail to take a stand when a hapless country gets ruthlessly bombed, your transformative purpose of improving the lives of human beings sounds hollow.

---

[2] All of these statements have been referenced from the company websites.

Let us go through a very interesting example. A bright young lady, went to Stanford to study chemical engineering. She initially wanted to go into medicine as she was inspired by her great-great-grandfather but she was scared of needles. She dropped out of Stanford to work on her own venture. She pioneered the technology where through a tiny drop of blood, medical conditions like high cholesterol and diabetes could be identified. No painful needles were required. The devices for this testing could be placed in every home. She raised hundreds of millions of dollars to scale her business. Her dream for the company was that, 'less people have to say goodbye to the people they love'. Very noble and very transformative.

She wanted to change the world of healthcare by putting in every home, devices that could take many tests through one drop of blood. She would often say to her employees, 'You are part of something that is going to change the world. What higher purpose is there?' She was known to be an excellent storyteller and was often termed the 'female Steve Jobs'. She marketed herself brilliantly—graced the covers of Fortune, Forbes and gave TED Talks. She became the world's youngest self-made female billionaire with a net worth of US$4.5 billion. Despite the transformative purpose, brilliant storytelling and exceptional marketing as an entrepreneur, there was one tiny problem with Elizabeth Holmes and her firm Theranos. Her technology didn't work and hence everything started falling apart.[3] She was charged with massive fraud by the Securities and Exchange Commission (SEC) in 2016. She has been

---

[3] The timeline of events has been documented very well here: https://www.businessinsider.in/tech/the-rise-and-fall-of-elizabeth-holmes-who-started-theranos-when-she-was-19-and-became-the-worlds-youngest-female-billionaire-before-it-all-came-crashing-down/articleshow/63859273.cms

found guilty on multiple fraud counts and is awaiting her sentence, which can go up to 20 years, in a few months.[4]

Storytelling is good, when it is backed up by integrity. When integrity is missing, storytelling can't do much for you. As an entrepreneur, having a transformative purpose and communicating that as the ultimate story is very powerful. But it is a double-edged sword. You should have the inner strength to talk the talk and walk the walk.

GO BIG ON THE 'ORIGIN STORIES'

One of the stories you should cultivate as an entrepreneur is the 'origin story', as in why did you start your company or start a brand. Such interesting anecdotes, if narrated well, can become a part of folklore and draw consumers in to your marketing stables. Most companies with high brand equity do this extremely well.

The pattern to most of the origin stories is the 3 act movie structure we discussed in Chapter 3, titled 'How Does Hollywood Use Storytelling'? A problem followed by the challenges followed by the resolution. Let us go through a few examples.

After the 1941 attack on Pearl Harbour, by the Japanese on the United States, the import of Coca-Cola syrup to Germany had to be stopped due to the logistics involved. Max Kieth, Coca-Cola's chief in Germany innovated and brought in another soda to cater to the German market.[5] Hope you are reading this book with a can of Fanta in hand. This origin story has been narrated again and again across many employee and consumer marketing forums.

---

[4] Let's see where this disturbing story goes: https://www.theguardian.com/technology/2022/jan/13/elizabeth-holmes-sentence-september-fraud

[5] Fanta used to be my favourite drink even when I was health conscious at one point in time: https://www.indiatimes.com/culture/who-we-are/8-big-companies-and-their-surprising-origin-stories-that-ll-change-the-way-you-see-them-276512.html

There is a very interesting origin story for a service that you may take for granted today. On a snowy night in Paris in 2008, two gentlemen shivered while they waited for a taxi. They didn't get one. One of them joked about ordering a private limo through an app. Over the course of time, it didn't turn out to be a joke.[6] Today, Uber founded by Travis Kalanick and Garrett Camp, operates in over 80 countries and provides a big relief to people like me who do not like to haggle with auto drivers every morning.

In 2011, two young smart guys wanted to build a photo sharing app. They didn't like the existing photo sharing apps as they were trying to make photos look prettier or more stylish. 'We wanted a place to share awkward selfies and funny photos with our friends', writes Evan Spiegel, on how Snapchat was founded. He goes on to write,

> 'And after hearing hilarious stories about emergency detagging of Facebook photos before job interviews and photoshopping blemishes out of candid shots before they hit the Internet (because your world would crumble if anyone found out you had a pimple on the 38th day of 9th grade), there had to be a better solution.[7]

Today, Snapchat has a market capitalization in excess of US$45 billion.[8]

Who are these origin stories best aimed at?

You? Definitely.

Consumers? Definitely.

Employees? Definitely.

---

[6] Link to the Uber story: https://looka.com/blog/famous-brands-origin-stories/
[7] I love this write-up on the genesis of Snapchat. Accurate, honest and to the point: https://newsroom.snap.com/lets-chat/
[8] Honestly, after a one billion dollar valuation, the rest is largely notional: https://companiesmarketcap.com/snap/marketcap/

You might be surprised to hear that such stories even resonate with investors. The general perception is that most investors are male, dry, obsessed with numbers and devoid of emotion. I have had the privilege, not sure if privilege is the right word, of interacting with and knowing many of them personally. And I can tell you they do get bored listening to pitches throughout the day that rattle out numbers and business model projections. They are desperate to latch on to a winning idea and want to get rid of the dryness in their lives. Storytelling actually works extremely well with investors also.

A good friend of mine, a renowned investor in India, once told me about an aspiring entrepreneur who got the entire group of investors in a boardroom interested by asking all of them a very simple question , 'How do you feel'? His story went along the following lines,

Imagine you are a young professional. Your purse is slightly tight. You, a lady, along with four other lady friends of yours, book a budget hotel in Goa, the party capital of India. The place seems fine on the internet. You land up there to have the time of your life. Once you enter the room, you find dirty bed sheets, a small cute baby cockroach in a corner, an old used razor in the toilet and a reception that doesn't answer your phone calls. How do you feel about it?

The entire room of dry and bored investors, once they started imagining this story, got hooked onto his presentation. They understood the pain point and the story depiction easily in their minds. And thus, they planned to invest in the budget hotel concept with a guaranteed level of service. I wanted to name the investor and the entrepreneur in this story but the investor asked me not to, as the other entrepreneurs he is invested in might get jealous and angry. Some entrepreneurs have a lot of self-confidence—like eggshells!

Some of you may have the question, do origin stories work only for massive brands or really global brands? The answer is no. Origin stories work for everyone.

Mavalli Tiffin Room (MTR) Foods, is a mid-sized food company in India. They are famous for making masalas and everyday spices. During the time of the Second World War, due to the shortage of rice, the cooks at MTR replaced 'rice', a key ingredient in the staple diet of 'Idli' with semolina and added a few veggies.[9] Today, 'Rava Idli' is a bestselling item that is prepared for breakfast across hundreds of millions of homes in India and this story is very famous.

You should craft a great origin story. Needless to say, it should be true and enthralling. Most consumers, including me, have a very strong bullshit detector ingrained in us.

COLOURS, IMAGES AND METAPHORS IN STORYTELLING

In the 1992 cricket world cup in Australia, Pakistan was looking at being knocked out early from the tournament. Their team, after a few initial losses and being saved by the rain, was clearly low on morale. In a must-win match against the mighty Australian team at home, Pakistan's talismanic skipper, Imran Khan, stepped out for the toss wearing, not the Pakistan team jersey, but a T-shirt with a tiger drawn on it. He wanted his young team, maybe slightly overawed and low on morale, to play like cornered tigers. He asked his team to fight like a cornered tiger because nothing is more dangerous than a cornered tiger. In a few weeks, Imran Khan had scripted one of the greatest turnarounds in cricketing

---

[9] One of my favourite brands in life. The origin story of MTR Rava Idli: https://theprint.in/pageturner/excerpt/bisibele-bath-to-rava-idli-how-bengalurus-mtr-mixed-tradition-and-innovation-perfectly/318892/

history and was getting ready to give his victory speech as the captain of the new world champions.[10]

If you recall, in Chapter 3, titled 'How Does Hollywood Use Storytelling', we looked at the incredible role of colours, metaphors and images that the world of movies employs as great storytelling techniques. The world of sports, in fact, is replete with such examples. Some of these metaphors are carefully used to hook the crowd to support you and maybe, scare the opponent a tad bit. Think of tennis legend Rafael Nadal's bottles that need to be placed correctly before he plays every point or cricketing legend Steve Waugh's red handkerchief which 'never let him down' on the big stage, which serve as excellent storytelling techniques.

Some entrepreneurs have very smartly used their power of dressing to build an outstanding story. Steve Jobs, founder of Apple and Mark Zuckerberg, founder of Facebook are famous for wearing black T-shirts and jeans on most days. Even Elizabeth Holmes, Theranos's founder, the story we just discussed a couple of pages back, mimicked her fashion style along the lines of Steve Jobs. While Mark Zuckerberg has often said that he doesn't want to spend mental bandwidth on choosing clothes, the reasons for going for black is a little more profound. In a subsequent chapter, we will look at what the colour black signifies. It is used in communication as a tool to convey slow but dramatic and permanent transformation. This fits exactly with the kind of purpose they are following for their companies. If you are students of mystical subjects in Hinduism, the colour black is associated with the planet Saturn conveying the same message of slow, dramatic and permanent transformation.

Similarly, other entrepreneurs follow a carefully curated dressing sense. Disgraced Indian liquor baron and ex-airline

---

[10] A very interesting recollection of the 'cornered tiger' incident: https://caravanmagazine.in/vantage/imran-khan-pakistan-1992-world-cup-squad

mogul, Vijay Mallya, referred to as the 'King of Good Times', during his heyday, would often be dressed in multiple styles ranging from the lighter pastels to the black suit. Very much in line with the companies he was running. The lighter pastels are often associated with luxury and optimism, qualities required for his line of businesses in aviation and liquor.

The founders of Indian technology giant, Infosys, were always communicating about their middle-class values. Hence, despite being billionaires, their dressing styles remained very middle class and never changed much, despite the unbelievable affluence that came their way.

One of the reasons why the legendary Indian stockbroker, Harshad Mehta caught the eyes of the regulators for supposed corruption was due to his expensive suits and his fondness for luxury cars, which became a metaphor attached with him. When regular people started losing money as the stock markets crashed, the metaphors associated with him actually brought his downfall.

Politicians do this extremely well in democracies like India. A poor citizen's leader will always be dressed as a poor citizen no matter how big he or she becomes. I am not taking names to avoid getting into trouble.

Similarly, if you are an entrepreneur, depending on your line of business, your dressing style should subtly communicate the same set of values. And if you can generate a metaphor through the repeated usage of words or a favourite pen or an interesting hand gesture or a witty line in an interview, you are going to be etched in people's minds.

In a panel discussion with legendary Indian businessman Ratan Tata, a lady in the audience asked him, 'What excites you the most?' In a lighter vein, Ratan Tata replies,

'That is the most difficult question you have asked this evening. How can I say that publicly?'

The audience, the ones watching it live and the millions who see it later, erupt and chuckle.

GENERATE BUCKETS OF EMPATHY

What sort of movies do we really like? The redemption story. The rags-to-riches story. The story where the hero wins against all odds. Think of movies like *The Pursuit of Happyness*, *Rocky*, *Moneyball* or even *M.S. Dhoni: The untold story*.

In fact, when the first trailer of the movie on legendary cricketer Mahendra Singh Dhoni was released, it highlighted the humble origins of the cricketer and how he served as a ticket collector on a railway station in India. The movie chronicled how he went on to fight insurmountable odds to become one of the greatest sportspersons the world has ever seen.

Why do these kinds of stories sell and endear themselves to millions of potential consumers? The answer is simple. Stories like these generate oxytocin, the main chemical behind empathy. You empathize with the protagonist and are invariably hooked onto them.

The Black Lives Matter movement, in recent history, that caught global attention, generated immense furore after an unarmed black man George Floyd was killed by Minneapolis police officer Derek Chauvin. Chauvin held his knee against Floyd's neck for more than nine minutes during an arrest in Minneapolis on 25 May 2020, as the 46-year-old repeatedly pleaded that he could not breathe.[11] When you hear of such an incident, there is rage and there is empathy for the victim. When millions feel it, there are widespread protests that move on to the streets.

---

[11] Reference to the gruesome incident: https://www.aljazeera.com/news/2022/4/28/derek-chauvin-appeals-murder-conviction-for-killing-george-floyd

Some entrepreneurs have very smartly played the empathy card. Elon Musk has often said in interviews that he sleeps on his factory floor,[12] he doesn't have a place to live in despite being the richest man in the world. He has often spoken about his failures with Space X.

'I don't even own a place right now, I'm literally staying at friends' places,' Elon Musk said during an interview with TED, 'If I travel to the Bay Area, which is where most of Tesla's engineering is, I basically rotate through friends' spare bedrooms,' he added.[13]

Indian IT services major, Infosys, had a rock star reputation in the 1990s and the 2000s due to the profile of the entrepreneurs. The seven founders of Infosys, all from middle-class families, with no big name backing them, with limited capital and just on the basis of their hard work, went on to build a global technology giant. Their story of scaling up globally on the basis of Indian middle-class values is an excellent entrepreneurial story.

The Tata Group, one of India's most respected conglomerates, has built an extraordinary level of consumer equity on the basis of the story that they never give or take bribes to do business. They are always fair in their dealings with everyone.

Interestingly, new-age entrepreneurs are making their presence felt a lot more in the media these days. On the first season of Shark Tank that premiered in India a few months ago, many young entrepreneurs came on air to portray their stories. One entrepreneur spoke about being brutally rejected when

---

[12] The richest man in the world sleeping on the factory floor: https://www.cnbc.com/2018/04/11/elon-musk-says-he-is-sleeping-on-tesla-factory-floor-to-save-time.html

[13] No place to stay for the richest man in the world: https://www.moneycontrol.com/news/trends/elon-musk-says-he-doesnt-own-a-home-crashes-at-friends-places-8374891.html

he started. Another one mentioned how he was broke when he started his entrepreneurial venture. A third entrepreneur spoke about the challenges of being a woman in an ecosystem that is male-dominated.

In the next chapter, we will also explore this topic of entrepreneur-led storytelling from a marketing perspective. It is a super interesting piece in case you have entrepreneurial dreams.

DON'T OBSESS WITH STORYTELLING

While some of you, after reading this chapter, may be under the impression that if you are an aspiring entrepreneur, you have to be a story-churning machine and a camera-facing marketer selling yourself all the time. While the spirit of the above statement is true, I should suggest that storytelling-led marketing is not the only way to become a billionaire. History is replete with examples of reclusive entrepreneurs who liked to stay away from the limelight.

Does the name Ingvar Kamprad ring a bell?

Ingvar Kamprad, a shipping magnate, was renowned for his reclusiveness along with his frugal ways. He founded the Swedish company which supplies furniture to your home and office, IKEA. His frugal ways included

> encouraging his staff to write on both sides of pieces of paper, berated them for leaving lights on and was all about cost-cutting in his private life too, choosing to drive a basic Volvo, only fly economy and shamelessly stock up on freebie salt and pepper sachets when he was eating out.[14]

In 2008, in line with his perceived stingy behaviour, he once admitted that he saved money by getting his hair cut when

---

[14] This story is from the internet. Like with most stories on the internet, I cannot vouch for its accuracy: https://www.lovemoney.com/gallerylist/87931/reclusive-superrich-people-from-howard-hughes-to-the-barclay-brothers

he visited poor countries. He told a Swedish newspaper: ‹Normally I try to get my hair cut when I'm in a developing country. Last time it was in Vietnam.'[15]

After reading this paragraph, I would have laughed about it but given the man has wealth in the excess of US$50 billion, I will treat it as life wisdom that only billionaires can teach you.

However, I think the 'reclusive entrepreneur' persona is more of an anomaly than the norm. The world is only getting tougher and more competitive, and the NOISE is increasing disproportionately every day.

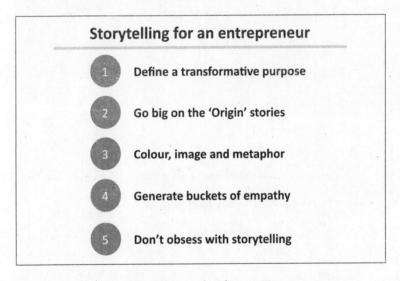

Figure 6.1: Storytelling Principles for an Entrepreneur

Remember, if you do not market yourself, the world will not do it for you (Figure 6.1).

---

[15] Totally opposite my personality. Maybe that's why I am not sitting on over US$50 billion: https://www.thesun.co.uk/news/5445832/ikea-founder-worth-54bn-volvo-flea-markets/

Stopping advertising to save money is like stopping your watch to save time.

Henry Ford, founder of Ford Motor Company

Marketing is like sex; everyone thinks they are good at it.

Steve Tobak, Author and Columnist

CHAPTER 7

CREATING LEGENDARY CONSUMER BRANDS

So welcome to possibly one of the more interesting chapters in this book.

Not that the other chapters are boring but marketing always appeals to everyone, from the douchebag to the rock star. To clarify, I am the douchebag and you are the rock star, if that makes you happy.

Irrespective of whichever decade we may live in, marketing and branding will always be necessary. From Henry Ford's time to marketing beautiful cars to potentially dating robots in the next 30 years, marketing and branding will remain a critical part of business and will retain their high sex appeal.

When we speak of marketing or branding, we implicitly speak about storytelling. No other chapter has storytelling so well ingrained as branding or marketing does.

In this chapter, I bring you a ringside view of how marketing might evolve and hence how the world of storytelling will.

PURPOSE-LED STORYTELLING ALL THE WAY

One of the big brand conversations that has been happening over the last few years and is likely to happen over the next decade is purpose. A brand purpose tries to answer the following questions:

What does a brand stand for?

What is its higher aim?

Why does the brand exist?

What do we, as a brand, want to do in the future?

Notice the word purpose is nothing but storytelling in its most obvious form. By using storytelling, human beings created concepts by which a large number of people could be brought under one roof with some shared ideals. Earlier it was religion and politics. Then it moved to the concept of a corporate, football club or pop culture references.

Now this notion has been extended to brands under the guise of purpose to bring consumers, vendors and employees under one roof with a shared ideal.

For instance, the purpose of Starbucks coffee is 'To establish Starbucks as the premier purveyor of the finest coffee in the world while maintaining our uncompromising principles while we grow'.

Some of you might think of purpose as the same thing as the mission statement of a company. I don't want to complicate it, but there is a slight difference. Purpose is part of the mission statement. The mission statement is about why I exist (purpose) and how I exist (values).

To be honest with you, even in academic circles, there is some confusion in the common understanding of the following terms—mission statement, purpose, values and vision. But in this chapter, I focus on the real-world practitioner's perspective.

An interesting question is why is 'purpose' becoming such a front and centre conversation for brands? Some hypotheses can be as follows:

Gen Z and millennial consumers increasingly care about what a brand stands for, what its impact on the communities is and how it treats its employees.

I personally think the book *Ikigai: The Japanese Secret to a Long and Happy Life*, published about 5 years ago, brought this purpose conversation to the forefront.

How does storytelling as part of purpose manifest itself? Let's take a look.

Starbucks launched a documentary series *Upstanders* that features stories of extraordinary courage. According to Howard Schultz, CEO of Starbucks, the short films cover stories of immigration, racism, drug abuse and poverty by focussing on extraordinary acts of courage across America. He also mentioned that the first season of *Upstanders*' episodes reached more than 60 million people.[1] This was particularly important as issues like Black Lives Matter and police brutality took over the common narrative in the United States around 2020. This is in line with Starbucks' purpose of maintaining its uncompromising principles while it grows.

Dove, Unilever's powerhouse brand, tries to live up to its purpose of 'to make a positive experience of beauty accessible to every woman'. To bring this to life, they try to bring real beauty in their ads and communication by using untouched photographs of real women and not models to reflect the true population.[2]

Using storytelling to drive purpose-driven marketing also manifests in what is termed moment marketing. Moment marketing is a technique used by brands to comment on trending news and events. They deploy witty lines and interesting videos to capture user attention.

One of the brands that does this the best is the Indian dairy brand, Amul. Amul, at its disposal, has a great storytelling

---

[1] Link to more details on the Upstanders series:https://mashable.com/article/starbucks-upstanders-season-2-original-series
[2] For more details on how Dove lives its purpose: https://deloitte.wsj.com/articles/how-unilevers-dove-delivers-on-its-brand-purpose-01589396530

icon, the Amul girl, who has excellent top-of-mind recall in India. The brand has often commented wittily on contemporary events.

Some examples are as follows:

When Elon Musk became the world's richest man, Amul came up with an image with a tagline, 'Richest Muska!' and 'Teslap it on'. 'Muska' besides referring to Musk, in Hindi also means butter, one of Amul's products. In addition, 'Teslap', besides being a reference to Tesla also wittily refers to 'slapping it on a toast', directly linked to their products, bread and butter.

When fuel prices started to shoot up in India, they came up with a witty ad which showed the Amul girl filling the fuel tank in her car with the tagline 'Painfuel increase' with the caption 'Affordable taste' referring to their products always being perceived as value for money.

Being associated with food and happy moments along with the Amul girl as a brand ambassador and witty storytelling helps Amul increase its top-of-mind recall.

The storytelling principle that is being extensively deployed here is the leveraging of popular culture references.

However, not everything is hunky-dory when it comes to purpose-led storytelling. Let us go through a very interesting example.

As part of its goals and ambitions, Hennes & Mauritz (H&M), the Swedish fast fashion clothing company, wanted to conduct business, 'in a way that is economically, socially and environmentally sustainable'.[3] As part of being socially responsible, H&M expressed concerns about alleged human rights violations against Uyghur Muslims in China's Xinjiang province and warned to stop using cotton from this region.

---

[3] This is being referenced from the company website: https://hmgroup.com/sustainability/leading-the-change/goals-and-ambitions/

What happened next sent shockwaves to global businesses trying to operate in China.

H&M was wiped off China's e-commerce sites, maps and social media platforms. Celebrities cut ties with the brand. There was a huge online boycott by Chinese citizens against H&M clothing. They were almost erased from the world's biggest consumer market overnight.

Purpose-led storytelling is a double-edged sword. This is especially true in global environments where only one system of human values doesn't prevail. Simple guidance for all brands is to stay off matters that seem ingrained with religion and politics.

STORYTELLING TO APPEAL TO YOUR SENSES

The first time when someone told me that there is this YouTube influencer who eats noodles live every day, has millions of viewers who log in to watch her eat noodles and she makes millions of dollars every month, I thought it was a massive joke. However, out of curiosity, I decided to Google a little more and came across the term *mukbang*, a combination of the Korean words *meongneun* and *bangsong* meaning eating and broadcast.

This trend is not new and has been prevalent for over a decade. What is characteristic about this trend is that the person eats a copious amount of food and the viewers find the sound of chomping, biting and swallowing therapeutic. This paragraph is not a typing error. Every word of what you are reading is FACTUALLY CORRECT.

I went on this YouTube channel called 'HunniBee ASMR' (refer Figure 7.1) with nearly 8 million subscribers as I write this chapter. By the time you read the book, she would have crossed 10 million subscribers. In her videos, she eats a variety of items—combs, keyboards, dish sponges, perfumes and bracelets all made from cakes and rice. The chomping is loud,

Who wouldn't want to make millions by eating everyday?

Figure 7.1: Videos from the HunniBee ASMR Channel on YouTube Where She Is Eating Boots, Bottles and Hairbrushes, Made from Edible Items Like Cakes, Etc. Do You Want to Try?

clear and aesthetic. Initially, I found the videos cringeworthy. But give it time and it grows on you. You will be surprised!

Whatever you might think, for heaven's sake, please do not eat the pages of this book and broadcast it live.

The larger point I am trying to make is that storytelling is going to become sensory oriented—with greater involvement of sight, smell, touch, hearing and taste. We have all traditionally believed that storytelling is about writing and speaking. It is actually much bigger than that. When you start narrating your stories appealing to the various senses, the impact is manifold. As the *mukbang* star's bank balance will tell you.

The basic question is why does storytelling targeting your senses work?

The answer is simple. It is about how your brain works.

More than 75 per cent of your decision making in your brain is controlled by the reptilian (instinctual) and the limbic (emotional) part of your brain. The reptilian part of the brain is related to primitive habits linked to thirst, hunger, everyday habits such as putting your phone for charging and so on. The limbic portion of your brain is involved in behavioural and emotional responses. These two parts of the brain are driven by emotion rather than rationality. These two parts of the brain are why you make irrational decisions while shopping. The sensory aspects of storytelling appeal to them directly and trigger them viciously.

To be honest, none of this is new. Scientists knew about how the brain works many decades ago. However, what is new is that technology can now send the right sensory stimuli to activate these centres of the brain. And in the future, more and more brands will only do this through their storytelling.

Let us take a few examples of how leading brands are doing this.

You would have heard about this term called autonomous sensory meridian response (ASMR). It basically translates to a set of sights and sounds that relaxes your brain. It is also termed brain massage.

In an attempt to promote relaxation, toy maker LEGO built a music album using 10,000 LEGO bricks and making them carefully clink against each other. The resultant noise is perceived to be relaxing to your brain.[4] Listeners can use this audio supplement before trying to go to sleep, after a stressful meeting or while taking a stroll in the park.

In case you have a young child at home, why don't you take away all of his/her LEGO bricks and start throwing them against each other everywhere. While the bricks might make a

---

[4] You should definitely try this: https://www.lego.com/en-in/aboutus/news/2021/february/white-noise

relaxing noise, your child's screams might not be so appealing to the ear.

In case you aren't sure about the idea, watch 'The Making of LEGO White Noise' on YouTube.

If you remember, in an earlier chapter, I spoke about a cafe in Shanghai that produces an audio sound through an attached speaker, and as a result, you think the coffee is sweeter than it actually is. It is seen as an innovative way to control your consumption of the biggest evil of our times, not liquor, cigarettes, drugs or oil, but sugar.

The retail industry across the world is bringing in sensory elements as a critical element in its storytelling.

Ikea, a multinational conglomerate that sells furniture in massively big outlets decided to bring in sensory storytelling in its Paris outlet. Paris, if some of you have been there, besides being beautiful, is famous for extremely small apartments. To bring this small-sized apartment concept to life, they built a store that doesn't mimic their traditional massive size but a significantly smaller size to replicate the typical Paris apartment.

The reason for this concept is that you as a consumer can visualize how real life can be in that store. This is classical storytelling where the right combination of chemicals—dopamine for focus, endorphins for joy and oxytocin for empathy—is being released in the brain as you try to imagine living there.[5]

Similarly, the hospitality industry is involving sensory elements as part of its marketing and storytelling narrative. According to a survey by InterContinental Hotels Group (IHG), global travellers agree that a good night's sleep is non-negotiable, but 80 per cent of them struggle with it. Hotels like Marriott through

---

[5] Very interesting concept in my view: https://about.ikea.com/en/about-us/ikea-retail/ikea-paris-la-madeleine-small-store

its Moxy Hotels chain have launched ASMR bedtime stories. As part of this series, guests will have access to 60-second stories to listen to in their bedroom to wind down after a long hard day.[6]

When you speak of storytelling through the senses of sight and hearing, the sense of smell cannot be forgotten. In the year 2017, to make your virtual experience a more lifelike one, Tokyo based start-up Vaqso, designed an emitter releasing a smell based on what you are watching in the VR sets.[7] Technology is no smelly matter after all!

All of these are part of a larger marketing theme of turning a product into a service. Like I wrote about it in an earlier chapter, eating a packet of chips is more than just ripping the packet open, stuffing the deep-fried potato into your mouth and throwing the packet away. With the element of sensory-led storytelling, you will appreciate the smell of the original potato, a rhythmic sound to help you eat less and appreciate more and make your enjoyment of chomping on deep fried potatoes a more memorable one.

You might like it so much that you might make your own *mukbang* videos and become a millionaire influencer.

THE FUTURE OF BRAND STORYTELLING IS INTERACTIVE

This is a no-brainer and this theme is not new by any stretch of imagination. But it is important to see how social media,

---

[6] You should consider staying here for sure: https://news.marriott.com/news/2019/04/11/moxy-hotels-launches-first-of-its-kind-a-s-m-r-bedtime-story-videos-exclusively-for-guests-of-the-new-moxy-nyc-chelsea

[7] Would you smell this gadget? https://www.businessinsider.in/tech/virtual-reality-gets-smelly-thanks-to-this-japanese-startup/articleshow/59345313.cms

the power of superfast internet and the metaverse are shaping interactivity.

Why is interacting with consumers for a brand so important?

Because, as a member of an audience, your brain wants to live in the story your brand is telling you about. Your brain wants to experience the joy, the tribulations and the new experience it will have by living in the brand story's ecosystem.

As a brand, if you want to hook people into being obsessed with your brand, you will make your storytelling interactive.

How has interactive storytelling evolved over the last decade? It is a very interesting journey.

The first time I experienced interactive storytelling is when I watched the hit Netflix series, *Black Mirror: Bandersnatch* at the end of 2019. It invited audiences to participate in the decision-making series and to choose among options the story would move in. According to the internet, there are five main endings to the story.[8] I have managed to see only two of them. How many have you seen?

When it comes to interactive storytelling, the world of movies always seems to push the bar higher.

You should consider seeing the interactive film *The Angry River* by Armen Perian. The movie has five different narrative journeys. Depending on where your interest lies, as understood by eye-tracking technology using your webcams, you will be shown one of the narratives.[9] Your sub-conscious

---

[8] How many endings have you seen to the series? https://www.thewrap.com/black-mirror-bandersnatch-netflix-5-main-endings-secret-kill-dad-movie-set-mom-pearl-ritman-coronavirus/

[9] Read some interesting aspects about this journey: https://www.forbes.com/sites/jessedamiani/2019/02/18/the-angry-river-is-a-landmark-interactive-film-now-armen-perian-is-pushing-the-form-even-further/?sh=1e8021a26f17

mind and how it perceives different characters will determine which narrative of the movie you will watch.

On why he made such a movie, Armen says, 'I knew I wanted to make a film where the audience's perception of the story was influenced by them—but I didn't want to take the viewer out of it with clicks, motions, prompts or the like.'

However, interactive brand storytelling is not a new phenomenon and has been active for more than a decade.

In 2011, Ogilvy and Mather created an interactive campaign for carbonated water brand Perrier. In its most basic concept, the advertisement is about an attractive lady walking into a nightclub. As the temperature gets hotter, the nightclub gets wilder and raunchier and her journey more memorable. How do you decide virtually if the temperature gets hotter? If more people start visiting the advertisements on YouTube.

As more and more people click and watch the video, you move up and watch a total of six ad campaigns as part of an interactive experience where each ad gets wilder and more memorable than the other. The ads have been estimated to have gained more than 10 million views in one month.[10]

Another element of interactive storytelling is to listen to questions from your consumers and create content around it. It builds a sense of humility, engagement and trust with your consumer base.

Hope Bagozzi, Director of Marketing, McDonald's Canada received a question on why McDonald's food looks different in advertising compared to what is presented at the store. She created a video where she actually showed how the McDonald's burgers are shot in the real world. One of the

---

[10] Some more details on the brand campaign: https://www.genwow.com/2011/07/interactive-perrier-video-gets-sexier-as-number-of-viewers-go-up.html

major differences is that they try to make the seasonings through mustard and ketchup more pronounced in the product photos which are generally hidden under the bun when you buy them. The video received 12 million views, 38,000 likes, zero dislikes on YouTube and loads of good-will.[11]

This principle of listening to your viewers and creating content is also applicable if you intend to be an influencer and are trying to build your personal brand.

Now, coming back to the future, let us look at how interactive storytelling is evolving.

Rival Peak, the latest game from developer Genvid technologies is a 24-hour reality show on Facebook. There are 12 animated characters who are fending for themselves in a forest. These characters and their courses of action can be decided by the viewers through live polls making the experience supremely interactive. Does this work? Well, let's take a look at a few numbers.

Over the course of its 12 weeks season, the show witnessed over 100 million minutes of watch time from its viewers.[12] You don't need me to tell you how good this number is! The formal term that is used for experiences like these is 'mass interactive live events' (MILE). Now you get why.

Major League Baseball (MLB) player Micah Johnson created the character of a young black boy who wants to be an astronaut named 'Aku' which he converted into a non-fungible token (remember NFT where the entire media is

---

[11] Link to the YouTube video where she answers the question on why the food looks different. A great viewing experience indeed https://www.youtube.com/watch?v=oSd0keSj2W8

[12] More details of this fascinating concept: https://variety.com/2021/tv/news/rival-peak-facebook-watch-end-1234937639/

digital and all the details of who was the original owner and who it has been sold to are always visible).

Aku has gone on to become one of the most loved characters in the NFT space. Moreover, 10- minute videos were released from the Aku stables and end viewers could buy those NFTs.[13] There were over US$2 million of sales in about 28 hours.[14] Interesting, isn't it?

If I create an NFT of the first chapter I ever wrote in my life, how many of you would be keen to bid millions of dollars and buy it?

INFLUENCER-LED STORYTELLING

In an earlier chapter, we discussed why influencer-led story-telling is becoming big and how it will become massive in the next few years. Some of the reasons we looked at were declining trust in traditional institutions like the government, declining trust in technology companies and celebrities. Remember the declining trust numbers in Chapter 4 titled 'Our World in the Next Few Years'?

Why is this behaviour happening?

Every consumer wants to be connected to someone who comes across like him/her. Consumers crave for authenticity and honesty. Your brain is very curious to know and visualize the life of the influencer by placing yourself in his/her shoes.

As I have written in Chapter 4 earlier, you don't want to listen to a celebrity talking about a brand's benefits only because they have been paid millions of dollars. This reeks of

---

[13] Great story isn't it? https://nftnow.com/news/diversity-in-nfts-micah-johnson-announces-the-final-chapter-of-aku/

[14] Here are the details of some numbers on Aku. Quite spectacular indeed: https://www.pendulummag.com/art/2021/2/27/aku-micah-johnsons-character-to-inspire-kids-to-dream-without-limits

hypocrisy at some level. You want the influencer to advertise the brand to you only if they believe in it and if they genuinely believe it to be in your interest.

Influencer-led storytelling is already becoming very big in parts of the world like China and South Korea and is scaling up in the United States. According to a Forbes article, consumers love live-streaming and listening to their favourite influencers with nearly 500 million plus people in China hooked on it.[15] Even in emerging countries like India, FMCG majors are attributing 25–30 per cent of their marketing spends to influencers and this number will only increase.[16]

In course of time, nearly half of all advertising budgets for consumer-centric companies will be influencer centric. And not just for big influencers with millions of followers but even nano and mini-influencers, people like you and me.

So as a brand, how will the influencer help you with storytelling? Once you the pick the right influencer, they will follow the 3-part storytelling structure in their content. The storytelling principle at play is essentially the 3-act movie structure we discussed earlier.

Part 1: Problem

Part 2: Challenge

Part 3: Resolution which your product or service should assist with.

All of this content will ideally be delivered in short form or in rare cases in long form. Influencers will leverage the

---

[15] Ridiculous growth of live-streaming and influencers in countries like China: https://www.forbes.com/sites/michellegreenwald/2020/12/10/live-streaming-e-commerce-is-the-rage-in-china-is-the-us-next/?sh=53f2ad436535

[16] Don't you love such stories? We all have such promising influential careers being an influencer: https://www.livemint.com/news/india/fmcg-firms-shift-ad-spends-to-influencer-marketing-says-duff-phelps-report-11604396058087.html

storytelling principles they are familiar with—ending matters, pop culture references, Rule of 3 and power of anecdotes.

Sounds fairly simple, isn't it? It actually isn't.

The big challenge is to pick the right influencer. Someone whose content and behaviour fits in with your brand. If you are selling high-end cosmetics and the influencer has partnered with another company selling cigarettes or alcohol, it can get very tricky. If you are selling high-end cosmetics, you cannot partner with an influencer whose channel is dedicated to street food even if they have tens of millions of followers.

Not only do you have to pick the right content match with the influencer, but you also have to be careful about the other brands they endorse because they do cast an indirect shadow on your brand.

More importantly, as Web 3.0 starts coming in, spends on influencers will rise disproportionately. Even micro and nano influencers, you and I, with followers in the range of 10,000–50,000 will be in big demand. With Web 3.0, there will be no intermediate platform to moderate content or currency. The influencer will directly engage with his or her consumers and bring in huge elements of interactivity with Web 3.0.

So this will scale up significantly over the next few years. Add a bit of cryptocurrency to sell merchandise and non-fungible tokens to sell your memories, and you can book the latest Audi in advance.

Try it! Seriously!

ENTREPRENEUR-LED STORYTELLING

Do you know what Tesla's marketing budget is? Take a guess. It should be a high number considering electric vehicles is a new industry and has premium pricing. What do you think its marketing budget might be? How many millions of dollars?

The right answer is zero. Yes, you read that right. It doesn't have a marketing budget.

How can such a company manage without advertising? True, it has a great customer experience. A great product. A happy set of customers.

All of that is true, but their biggest marketing asset is Elon Musk.

Elon Musk has a social media following in excess of 80 million on Twitter as I write this chapter. He is charismatic, controversial, honest, witty, cryptic and many more things as the brand ambassador for Tesla.

The reason consumers like entrepreneur-led storytelling is simply because it is different and interesting. Every consumer is bombarded with so many ads that their brain switches off at one point. Given Musk is an excellent storyteller, he has his legion of followers hooked on every tweet of his. Every consumer wants to be in his shoes and understand what his world might appear like. His personality is far more attractive to consumers that the nuts and bolts of his company.

The storytelling principle at play is the power of popular culture (Musk is the ultimate popular culture icon) and how the power of anecdotes (his tweets) is more powerful than an underlying layer of hard numbers (the annual reports).

To be honest, this trend is not new. A lot of diehard Apple consumers, including me, had a similar curiosity about Steve Jobs. Steve Jobs was half the brand. His statements created ripples. Although Apple did have a sizeable marketing budget, their real brand ambassador was Jobs.

Similarly, the Tata Group in India, which enjoys enormous goodwill, has carefully harnessed stories around its first-generation entrepreneur, Jamsetji Tata, to build a hook and an indelible mark in consumers' minds.

There are many companies that are creating documentaries made on their founding families to tap into entrepreneur-led storytelling. This trend, called alternate advertising, is likely to scale up as consumers enjoy the storytelling journeys of the founders of the brands they love.

Why should this strategy work?

Because you will happily listen to the entrepreneur's personal journey rather than watch another ad among thousands of other ads. While watching such a journey or engaging with the CEO on social media, your brain is fully engrossed in trying to put yourself in the CEO's shoes and visualize their life.

The Founder, released in 2016, was a movie chronicling how American salesman Ray Kroc meets the owners of McDonald's and decides to turn it into the biggest restaurant business in the world.

While the movie received a mixed response at the box office, the reasons for that are not attributed to the story but potential budgetary constraints.[17] As a concept, it had tremendous potential. On IMDB, it has a rating of 7.2/10.0 with over 145,000 ratings.

To be honest, an entire book can be written on storytelling and brands.

There are implications in packaging for example. On how companies use colours, logos and refill bottles to drive their storytelling messages. Maybe I will touch upon it in my next book.

---

[17] Here is an interesting take on why 'The Founder' didn't live up to its potential: https://decider.com/2017/02/24/the-founder-flop-the-weinstein-company-michael-keaton/

Branding and storytelling in the future

#1 Purpose led storytelling all the way... although with a few hiccups

#2 Storytelling to appeal to your senses

#3 The future of brand storytelling is interactive

#4 Influencer led storytelling

#5 Entrepreneur led storytelling

Figure 7.2: Storytelling Themes for Branding in the Future

However, as we come to the end of this chapter (refer Figure 7.2 for a quick summary), the following is a massive RED FLAG to be cognizant about.

While marketing and storytelling go hand in hand, it is very critical to not go overboard and propagate a fake narrative.

A business leader I have worked with was dying to 'sell the story' that his region, India, was the fastest growing region in the world. While he generated a lot of traction with the global CEO, a few months later, people realized that something wasn't right.

It turned out that the Indian market itself was growing so fast that everyone in that market was growing at that high rate and he in fact was losing market share. His competitors in India were growing much faster than him.

Some of his actions didn't help either. He stopped subscribing to the quarterly reports that commented on market share to propagate his story about India.

In case the market share numbers were released, it would be very obvious he was a laggard when it came to performance in the Indian market.

Storytelling or not, integrity in life always comes first.

Be a good storyteller but also be high on integrity.

*Business opportunities are like buses;
there's always another one coming.*

Richard Branson, British billionaire,
entrepreneur and the man who went to space

*If you keep talking, I'm gonna start billing you,
and my time runs a thousand dollars an hour.*

Harvey Specter, Do you seriously want me
to tell you who Harvey Specter is?[18]

---

[18] Harvey Specter is one of the most iconic characters from the hit legal drama series 'Suits'. In case you haven't seen it yet, I strongly recommend you do it.

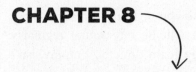

CHAPTER 8

DRIVING B2B CORPORATE SALES

Is B2B corporate sales important? Well, the simple answer is yes and the complicated answer is a resounding yes.

If you want to excel at any of the following careers and get your dream corner office, you need to be good at sales. When I say sales, you will need to get business from other corporates. The careers where you need to be good at selling to other corporates are as follows:

Management consulting

Strategy consulting

Technology consulting

Advisory services

IT services

Advertising

Corporate strategy teams in large companies and not to forget the world of legal services if you want to become Harvey Specter himself.

If you are trying to sell your product or service to another company, you are in the business of B2B corporate sales. A large portion of your success will be defined by the amount of business you can bring in from your clients who are not going to be individual consumers, like you or I but instead be large or small companies. And you will be interacting regularly with the CEO or the leadership team directly. Yummy, isn't it?

Is B2B Corporate sales likely to grow in the years to come? The answer is an emphatic yes. As economies grow and become more complex, companies will need more support from advisory services and hence B2B corporate sales is going to rise steadily. Think consulting. Think law. Think technology.

In this chapter, I am going to speak from my experience in a leadership role in management consulting for over a decade. The reason management consulting is often considered the gold standard of B2B sales is because it always has the ear of the CEO and the leadership team and the methods used by consulting firms are often world-class.

There are numerous applications of storytelling in B2B sales and we will explore what works and what doesn't in the next few pages.

CLEAR PROBLEM DEFINITION

Honestly, this is common sense. You need to define the problem well. Is problem definition important? Chapter 3, titled 'How Does Hollywood Use Storytelling', will tell you that if the problem is not defined clearly, the whole movie is not a pleasurable experience to watch. You don't need the world of movies to tell you that problem definition is important. Your 6-year-old child can provide that insight to you.

But the corporate world is a tad more COMPLEX.

Let me give you a couple of examples from my own experience in engagements I have personally led.

We want to be future-ready.

We want to be consumer-centric.

The above two are problem statements that were given by the leadership team for two major conglomerates when I started a transformation journey for them. To be fair, if you are in B2B sales, making your clients future-ready or consumer-centric are the most common problem statements that you will come across in your life.

How can the above problem statements go wrong? To start with, it is not because of bad intent but because of different interpretations.

'Consumer centricity' means different things for different people. It might mean brand loyalty for the marketing head. It might mean employee loyalty for the HR head. It might mean loyalty from retailers for the sales head. It gets even more complicated. The marketing head might believe you need to be 'consumer-centric' in the newer channels. The older channels are working fine anyway. The CEO might believe you have to be consumer-centric in all channels. The strategy head might believe you should target a 3-year time period to be fully consumer-centric. The sales head might believe you have to be consumer-centric from tomorrow.

Similarly, when you speak about being 'future ready', every leader has his own version of the future. Being ready for the future means different things for different people and is open to massive interpretation.

How does the world of Hollywood sort this out for you? They dedicate the first 15 to 20 per cent of the movie or the web series or Act 1 to hammer the message on clear problem definition. When Patrick Jane in *The Mentalist* arrives at the murder scene, the problem statement is very clear. He is trying to catch the murderer and bring justice to the deceased. The perennial chase for justice is clearly shown in the trailer of the episode. It is written against the description of the episode. The ambiguity in defining the problem is removed completely.

How can you use this clarity in problem definition from the world of Hollywood to the world of CEOs?

You can follow the following construct to clearly define the problem. The first step is to define the boundary conditions and the next step is to define the core problem.

Defining the boundary conditions involves making one of the following choices so that the scope of discussion is clearly explained. Think of it as drawing a boundary around the potential canvas you want to operate in.

Region: Is this programme applicable to a state, a country or the global business?

Channel: Is this programme applicable for newer channels, traditional channels or all channels?

Product or Service: Is this programme applicable to one product line, a few product lines or all product lines?

Time: Is the desired outcome to be achieved in 1 year, 2 years or 5 years?

Once the canvas for the problem has been marked out, it is important to define the core metric along with the start and end states.

In the case of consumer centricity, it might be the Net Promoter Score (NPS) and you might want to move it from 25 per cent to 50 per cent. NPS broadly implies how likely you are to recommend the product or service to a friend.

However, you cannot use a metric to define the core problem every time. And you might have to use a few sentences to define it.

For instance, in the case of trying to make your client future-ready, the word 'future' might imply,

Zero paper usage

A sales team that can cross-sell multiple products

All decision flow should be through the technology system

Payment turnaround cycles to be reduced to 48 h

How do you effectively use this problem definition with your CEOs and the leadership team? You put them on a slide and ensure it is the first slide in the first few meetings so that all of them are aligned to what you are trying to achieve. If there is any disconnect, it is sorted straightaway as shown in Figure 8.1.

POWER OF ANECDOTES

How can you show your credentials in a presentation pitch? There are multiple ways to do it. You can have a slide with the logos of all the companies you have worked for. If you have a lot of logos, this can be impressive. Or you can have a

Boundary conditions	Problem statement
Region: India	
Product: All products	Become consumer-centric as a firm
Channel: Emerging channels	Metric: Net Promoter Score *From 25% today to 50% in 1 year*
Time: 1 year	

Figure 8.1: Describing a Problem Statement Clearly. Show This Slide Multiple Times to Various Stakeholders in the First Few Discussions to Avoid Issues Later On

slide saying our clients have seen a numerical business benefit, say 8 per cent growth, on average. Or you can have a 60-s testimonial of another client CEO describing the problem, what you did and your impact.

The time spent by your client leadership on each of the three slides will be about 1–2 minutes. But which one do you think will stick in their minds?

To be fair, all three approaches have their utilities. If a preread is being sent where the client leadership is going to skim through the slides, a slide of all the logos can be helpful. If you are sitting in an airport lounge with the CEO with a lot of noise around, the slide on the average benefit your clients have seen historically has its utility.

However, if you are sitting with the entire client leadership team and they have given dedicated time to you, I have no doubt that a 60-s video testimonial from your previous client engagement works like magic. I have seen this repeatedly play out in my career.

Why do you think this happens?

What aspect of storytelling is at play here? Well, the power of anecdotes, where your brain prefers one powerful anecdote to a bunch of numbers is at play here.

If you need to take this testimonial approach upward by a notch, you can deploy the following tactic. Have a strong testimonial towards the beginning to bring in credibility and have another strong testimonial towards the end to leave on a high note. This is Nested Anecdotes at play. Also, your brain largely remembers the entire experience by the ending. The nested anecdote and a sound ending will hook your client's brain into your pitch.

Needless to say, if you are planning to leave a key testimonial at the end, you should plan your time well so that the audience has enough time to see it, absorb it and even ask a couple of questions about it.

But the two testimonial theory has always held me in excellent stead especially when I have presented to boards of large clients. You should try it too. You won't be disappointed. A combination of nested anecdotes and a peak at the end is a magical selling tool.

PAINT THE FUTURE

One of the most powerful tools in selling a piece of work is to paint the future for the client leadership team.

For instance, if the problem statement is that your client is losing orders and providing a poor service to their retailers because multiple sales executives selling different product lines are going to the same retailer and creating a mess after that, you may try the following.

The problem today, as indicated in Figure 8.2a, is that James goes to the store manager, Natasha, to enquire if she wants to look at the latest batch of washing machines. She says she doesn't need washing machines for now, but she is curious to learn about the new range of microwaves their company has launched.

As James is not selling microwaves and his colleague is, he doesn't enquire about the specifications. He takes down her request on his phone. At the end of a busy day, he forgets to mention this to his colleague. This results in lost sales and a poor experience.

Now the problem statement is to enable cross-sell, meaning that the same sales executive is now selling all product lines to the retailer rather than just one. This also means he can now cover a smaller number of retailers as he needs to spend more time per retailer.

Figure 8.2a: The Situation Today When Multiple Salesmen Selling Different Product Lines Visit the Same Store

Let us shift to the future, as shown in Figure 8.2b. James is now handling all products. Natasha again asks for microwaves. In this case, he not only asks her about the specifications but also shows her the product launch videos for the latest batch of microwaves. Seemingly happy, Natasha orders three more batches.

Which principle of storytelling is at play here? The 'Power of Anecdotes' where you are tempting the brain of your client leadership team to be engrossed in James' and Natasha's exchange is at play here. Dopamine is the chemical that is being released here in abundance.

Give this method a try. It is extremely powerful and effective. If you are feeling creative, bring in popular culture characters to have the conversation. Batman is my perennial favourite.

In the future

> Hi Natasha, do you want to take a look at our new line of washing machines?

> Hi James, I don't right now. But can you send me the latest line of microwaves?

James, Sales Executive, selling washing machines & microwaves for his company

Natasha, Store Manager

James is in charge of microwaves also now. He asks Natasha on the specifications she is looking for. He even shows her some of the videos of the latest microwaves on his tablet. She is very happy and orders for 3 more batches of microwaves.

Figure 8.2b: The Situation in the Future When the Same Sales Executive Covers All Product Lines at the Retailer Deriving the Benefits of Cross-Selling

You could try actors, movie characters or even cartoons. You are now tapping into the 'Power of Pop Culture References' in storytelling.

MAGICAL RULE OF 3

A key element in any sales pitch is how will you solve the problem?

What are the steps you will undertake?

What are your deliverables?

What are the outcomes you are targeting?

In one line, what is your approach going to be?

I once worked with a senior partner whose advice was to make the approach slide as busy as possible. Put in so much text that it looks complicated. His underlying theory was that if you can't convince the client leadership team, confuse them. If a slide has 10,000 words written on it, someone will think that it must be pretty darn good. Does this approach work? To some extent, it does.

However, an even better way to answer the approach question is not by confusing the client leadership team but by communicating in a simple manner so that they get it. I do believe that if you are reading this book, you want to make your career by believing in the power of your content, rather than trying to confuse the client CEO.

The approach slide in Figure 8.3 is very easy to understand and a fairly nuanced one to show to your client CEO. You have

Approach towards the program

1. Diagnostic	2. Identifying solutions	3. Prioritise and pilot
<Step 1>	<Step 1>	<Step 1>
<Step 2>	<Step 2>	<Step 2>
<Step 3>	<Step 3>	<Step 3>
Deliverables		
Identifying 'As Is' issues basis benchmarking	Conceptualizing a 'long-list' of potential solutions	List of prioritized pilots and execution plans

Figure 8.3: A Simple and Easy to Understand Approach Slide. Do You Want to Give This a Try?

3 stages in the overall programme—a 'diagnostic stage' to identify the issues, an 'identifying solutions stage' to identify all possible solutions and a 'prioritizing and piloting stage' to prioritize these solutions and execute the most impactful ones. Under each stage, you write 3 key steps you plan to undertake. And at the end of the programme, you have a set of 3 key deliverables. Not 75.

Besides being a very lucid, neat slide, this approach has an impact because it leverages the 'Power of 3' from the principles of storytelling. With less than 3 elements, your brain struggles to form a pattern to remember it while with more than 3 elements, it becomes tiring for your brain to process it.

Now some of you might have the temptation to write that fourth step because you believe it is likely to change the world. You might want to avoid that urge in case you want to drive impact with your client CEO.

But if you want to be like the senior partner I referred to earlier, you may go ahead.

Postscript: The senior partner was asked to leave, as he couldn't perform because he wasn't able to cultivate relationships with client CEOs. Do you wonder why?

EMBRACE MINIMALISM

The big question is when you are going in for your first meeting with the client leadership team, how many slides should you carry.

You might not be sure of the entire context.

You might not be sure if there is an actual requirement for your services.

Or you might be going in for your final meeting where you have a complete understanding of the context and the problem statement.

So how many slides should you show?

In my view and I know a lot of consulting partners will shiver to death at this answer, you shouldn't have a presentation of more than 10 slides. Yes, you read that right. 10 slides.

At my peak, I wouldn't even carry slides. I would draw what I wanted to say on a sheet of paper or on my iPad and show it to the client CEO.

So what should the 8–10 slides answer when you go in for your pitch meeting?

Following are some questions you can consider.

Who are you? We sell cloud services to mid-sized companies. Here are 3 points about our background.

What pain points do you solve? We help clients who are worried about excessive investments required to upgrade their IT infrastructure.

Where have you done it? A list of logos and a powerful client testimonial. One at the beginning and keep one for the end.

How do you do it? An approach slide with 3 stages, 3 steps in each stage and 3 key deliverables

Why are you better than the competition? 3 key points.

The above content shouldn't take you more than 8–10 slides. This is a true minimalistic presentation and hits the main points so that during the remaining time you can have a quality conversation with the CEO or the chief information officer (CIO) on what they are actually looking for.

I will take this forward and say no matter what stage of life you are in, you should never carry more than 8–10 slides to a meeting. If your discussion is extremely numerically heavy, carry an appendix but never more than 8–10 slides in the main presentation.

The reason minimalism works is that it removes the flab and forces the brains of everyone in the room, yours and your CEO's to focus on the issues that matter.

To be honest, was I always like this? The answer is no.

One of the (good) senior partners I worked with tried to change my thinking. I am grateful to him for everything he taught me. His words to me were,

'Trust me; you can compress all your messages into 8 slides. If the iPhone concept document, the World War 2 updates and Steve Job's resume can be written in 1 page, I am sure this pitch can be done in 8 slides'.

Quite profound, I think. Don't you (refer Figure 8.4)?

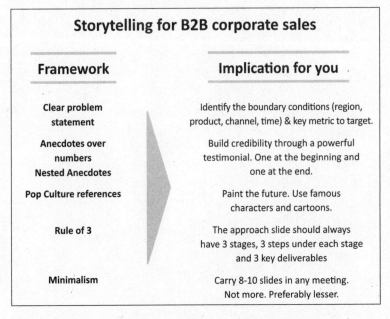

Figure 8.4. Impact of Storytelling on B2B Corporate Sales

PART 3

STORYTELLING FOR PERSONAL GROWTH

How can you create brilliant presentations
using storytelling?

How can you use storytelling to make
your audience retain what you are saying?

How do you become a master orator
using storytelling?

How can you excel in interviews
using storytelling?

How can you create your personal
brand using storytelling?

For my presentation today, I will be reading the
PowerPoint slides word for word.

Anonymous on the internet

I hate the way people use slide presentations
instead of thinking. People would confront
a problem by creating a presentation. I wanted them to
engage, to hash things out at the table,
rather than show a bunch of slides. People
who know what they are talking about
don't need PowerPoint.

Guess who, the man who created the
phone half the population uses.

CHAPTER 9

CREATING BRILLIANT PRESENTATIONS

When I conduct storytelling sessions, I often ask the participants a question about a memorable presentation they have come across in their lives. Invariably, the 2007 iPhone launch by Steve Jobs is often in the top three answers given. True, that launch presentation can be seen as one of the most pivotal moments over the last 20 years. It is equally mesmerizing when viewed even today. In case you haven't seen it, I would strongly encourage you to do so.

The follow-on question I ask is, 'what aspect of that presentation appeals to you so much'?

Answers from participants revolve around besides being an excellent orator, the slides used by Steve Jobs were extremely powerful in that presentation. The slides were minimalistic, uncluttered, had large fonts and had one message per slide. The slides weren't distracting the audience from the protagonist which wasn't the iPhone but Steve Jobs himself.

Guy Kawasaki, American author, venture capitalist and someone who worked with Steve Jobs in the early days of Apple to market the first line of Macintosh computers in 1984, has mentioned in various interviews that Steve Jobs liked large fonts, least number of words on a slide and practiced minimalism to the core.[1]

While all of us assume storytelling is synonymous with great oratory ability, a large part of storytelling is about the aids that you will use in the form of slides. You will create slides no matter which profession you are in or which stage of your career you are at. You will create slides if you are an entrepreneur, a venture capitalist, a technology guru, a management consultant, a corporate leader, a student, a bureaucrat, an influencer and surprise, surprise, even an author.[2]

Presentations, as slides, are becoming even more important as we move to the hybrid way of working. On a virtual call, the slide takes 80 per cent of the screen space while your face is in a tiny corner. Sometimes, your client might ask you to send the slides over to them, and they will evaluate what you have to say basis the slides. No face-to-face physical or virtual conversation is required.

Some of you might ask what can go wrong in a set of slides. Fair question.

From my experience, having held leadership positions in FMCG and in consulting, the following are some of the common mistakes that happen while creating slides for presentations.

The text is too small. It is difficult to read. (Thankfully, this book is written in a good font size)

---

[1] One of the interesting articles on Guy Kawasaki reminiscing about Steve Jobs - https://www.businessinsider.com/steve-jobs-used-190-point-text-on-presentation-slides-2019-4?IR=T

[2] In case you are wondering why I as the author of this book needed to create slides, ask yourself how the illustrative slides in each chapter have been created. In fact, this chapter in itself might have more than a dozen illustrative slides. Or, around that number.

Not enough detail or too much detail is there. Yes, too much detail can be a problem.

There are too many slides.

The narrator has been crippled due to the slides.

The slides are not customized for an audience.

The slides are just downright boring.

You don't get the crux of what they are trying to say.

The sentences are too long. It feels like I am reading a legal document.

One of the big mistakes that can be made by a presenter, as pointed out by *Harvard Business Review*[3] is to read the same information that is available on that slide. Not only is it less impactful as you are experiencing the same information twice, but it is downright cringeworthy. In some geographies like Europe, some business leaders can consider it an insult if you read the same material that is present on the slide or have sent it earlier as a pre-read.

In the next few pages, I will take you through some storytelling principles on how to create a great presentation document. Also to make it clear, these principles do not apply to just PowerPoint presentations but even Word documents and even Excel sheets. For instance, companies like Amazon rarely use PowerPoint presentations but are big fans of Word documents to carry their day-to-day stories and findings.

LEARN TO SAY 'I HATE YOU' PROPERLY

Every good consultant has gone through a training on a communication principle called the Pyramid Principle, created by Barbara Minto. It is a tool for storytelling to create maximum

---

[3] Read without fail: https://hbr.org/2013/06/how-to-give-a-killer-presentation

Dear Shirley,

Remember last Saturday afternoon when I was playing in the park with my boyfriend and you came over, and he told me that when my back was turned, you kissed him?

And also, on Sunday when you came to my house and my Mom made you a tuna fish salad for lunch and you said: "Yech! That's the worst salad I ever ate!"?

And yesterday, when my cat brushed against your leg, you kicked her and threatened to sic your dog "Monster" on her?

Well, for all of these reasons, I hate you, and I no longer want to be your friend.

Lucy

Figure 9.1: Shirley Is One Nasty Friend, Isn't She? Do You Have Friends Like Shirley in Real Life?

Source: https://www.dbai.tuwien.ac.at/staff/gatter/work/051104_The_Minto_Pyramid_Principle.pdf

impact. Let me bring this principle to life for you. Do spend a couple of minutes going through the images in Figures 9.1 and 9.2.

In the above illustration,[4] Lucy is miffed with her close friend Shirley and is trying to convey her angst to Shirley. Her first point of angst is Shirley's overtures towards her boyfriend. Her second point is Shirley's lack of appreciation towards her mother's tuna fish salad and her third point is against Shirley's behaviour towards her cat. A reasonable mind would say that when you are conveying a conclusion, you should elaborate

---

[4] The example has been referenced from The Minto Pyramid Principle, or the case for hierarchically structured thinking and communication, https://www.dbai.tuwien.ac.at/staff/gatter/work/051104_The_Minto_Pyramid_Principle.pdf

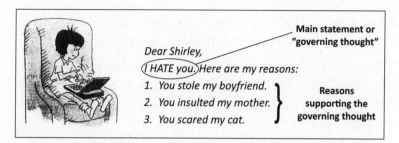

Figure 9.2: Is This How You Talk to Your Friends? Maybe You Should If You Have Friends Like Shirley

Source: https://www.dbai.tuwien.ac.at/staff/gatter/work/051104_The_Minto_Pyramid_Principle.pdf

on the data points first and then arrive at the conclusion to soften the blow or show method in a line of reasoning.

Right? Absolutely not.

As per the pyramid principle, you should get to the point first and then give the supporting arguments. The primary reason is the limited attention span of most of your audience members. The storytelling principle of minimalism is at play here to get to the point first and to cut out the flab. Also, when you are presenting to business leaders, they assume you have the necessary rigour and hence you should get to the point much faster. This is a principle we will extensively refer to in the rest of the document.

When Lucy tells Shirley, 'I HATE you. Here are my reasons', it is an exaggerated situation to comically explain this concept. To be crystal clear, never try this principle on your spouse while telling him or her what is wrong. IT IS BOUND TO FAIL.

I do not want to get a bad name because of your poor judgement.

THE EXECUTIVE SUMMARY

Imagine you walk into an elevator and you have Elon Musk enter the elevator with you.

Yes, the world's richest man and one of the world's most innovative entrepreneurs in the same lift as you.

You say, 'Hi!' out of admiration. He politely says 'Hi!' He is headed to the 25th floor. You are headed to the 26th floor. You try to strike up a conversation. He asks you what you are working on.

That should ideally freeze you in terror. The richest and the most visionary man in the world is asking you what you are working on. You have 30 seconds till he gets to his floor. What should you tell him?

This is the classical elevator pitch at play. How do you convey your entire work in less than a minute? Why do you need to compress your entire work in 30 seconds? Not just because the elevator will reach Elon Musk's floor but also because senior leaders or consumers have very low attention spans. If you beat around the bush, you will invariably lose them.

How do you get past this then? It is actually very simple. Summarize your entire work into 3 key points. One point could be the problem. One point could be the approach. One point could be the impact.

For instance, if Elon Musk asked me what I am working on, my answer would be along the lines of,

I am working on a book on 'business storytelling' as I think storytelling is going to be one of the most important skill sets of the upcoming decade and not enough attention is being given to it.

My book explores the world of psychology, movies and human evolution to identify storytelling principles and tells how they can be applied to corporates and individuals.

The book is currently doing very well and is close to selling a million copies.

Let's hope the last statement comes true. You are playing a very big part in achieving it.

Writing the executive summary is a very tricky exercise. If you notice, the Rule of 3 from the principles of storytelling is at play here. The pyramid principle of getting to the point first is also at play here.

When you create any document, you should ask yourself, what are the three most important points I am trying to convey? To be honest, it is easier said than done and can take years, if not decades of practice.

I should add that an executive summary is not a collection of screenshots of the subsequent slides in that section. The objective of the executive summary is to force you to think more clearly, not less.

CREATING AN EFFECTIVE DOCUMENT STRUCTURE

Let me start with a series of questions. Before you move forward, try to put your answers against the following questions.

How many slides should there be in a document?

How many slides should you present to your audience?

Shouldn't you be analytically rigorous while presenting to your audience?

Won't your audience be thrilled to see a 200-slide document?

Shouldn't the objective be to showcase all your work in a forum?

Let me tell you the answers I get when I ask these questions in a storytelling workshop. To some extent, I am going to exaggerate the responses to make a larger point.

We should keep as many slides as needed to showcase our work in the best manner.

It is criminal not to show the work we have done.

Our audience would love to read the analysis on 200 slides with gusto and enthusiasm.

If your slides are good, your audience will have a lot of attention to listen to 28–30 slides.

You get the gist of where I am headed. Storytelling principles like minimalism and the pyramid principle introduced earlier are the biggest principles that should be remembered while creating an effective document structure.

Why? It is simple. The human mind, honestly, can't listen to a narrative, written or spoken, in general, for more than 20 minutes. That's why the lovely TED Talks you listen to are always in the range of around 15 minutes.

No matter how lovely your analysis is or no matter how many footnotes of the sources of data you may have, you have 20 minutes to make your point to your audience's mind. After 20 minutes, the ability to retain and appreciate reduces significantly. Going forward, the attention spans of the next generation are reducing further. Need proof? Look at the phenomenal rise of TikTok and Instagram Reels.

So what is the right document structure?

Let me start with Guy Kawasaki's take on this. If you remember, as I mentioned a few pages earlier, he is, besides being a blockbuster venture capitalist and author, one of the earlier employees at Apple marketing the Macintosh computer in 1984. This book, incidentally, has also been typed on a MacBook.

He believes a document should have less than 10 slides and not cross more than 20 minutes in delivery. I fully concur.

Some of you might have the view that 10 slides are not enough to portray the gamut of work or nuance you may have. Well,

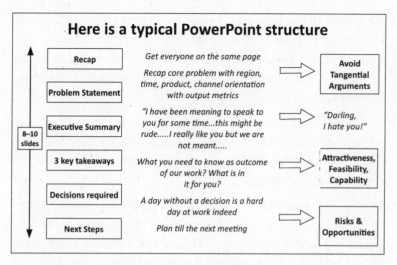

Figure 9.3: An Ideal Document Structure

that may be true. And hence the 10 most important slides should be in the main presentation while the rest can be in the Appendix section which may be used if a question is asked by someone in the room.

Again, so what is the ideal document structure? (Figure 9.3)

An ideal document structure starts with one recap slide summarizing the key points of the previous meeting in case the current discussion is a continuation of a long series of meetings. This is equivalent to a short recap at the beginning of any TV series. In case the current meeting is the first one, then this slide becomes optional.

For instance, in the last meeting, we kick-started our pro-gramme last week and we undertook research to identify the reasons why the turnaround time for complaints is 96 hours.

The next slide should be the problem statement slide capturing the problem statement, target metric and the dimensions of channel, region, product and time. You will recall from

Chapter 5 titled 'Driving Change' or Chapter 8 titled 'Driving Corporate B2B Sales' that a majority of problems in B2B sales or large transformation programmes are often because the problem is not clearly defined and every stakeholder thinks of the problem from their perspective.

For instance, the problem statement, in this case, could be improving customer experience by reducing turnaround time from 96 hours to 24 hours over the next 1 year across all channels and products.

Ideally, the next slide is optional, but I think it conveys clarity in thinking. The executive summary is a summary of key points on one simple page. This is the elevator pitch with Elon Musk that I was referring to in the previous section.

For instance, our research indicates 3 main problems,

1. Lack of interconnected manual communication systems leading to a delay in cycle communication

2. Incentives of account managers owning the account not incorporating turnaround time or customer satisfaction score

3. Not enough governance mechanisms to escalate to leader-ship in case turnaround time crosses 24 hours in a system

Remember from the pyramid principle, it is important to talk about the conclusions first rather than the methodology and the approach. Ideally, you should have one slide for each takeaway to elaborate on it in detail. For instance, in this example, we could have one detailed slide for each of the above three points.

Ideally, most leaders, in a meeting want to take decisions. Should they invest? Should they not invest? A slide capturing the decisions that they need to take also makes a lot of sense.

For instance, the decisions we need immediately are,

1. To change the appraisal metrics for account managers
2. Establishing the governance framework to report turn-around times and set up an escalation matrix immediately

And finally, a slide in terms of what is likely to happen next. It gives a flavour of the next steps and continuity if it is a long-term journey.

For instance, the next steps include detailing the appraisal metrics and setting up the governance framework over the next 45 days.

This entire structure is about 8–10 slides and can be used extensively across presentations. It is intuitive, simple and highly effective. The storytelling principles of minimalism, rule of 3, pyramid principle all come to life with this structure.

If you need more slides, they should ideally be in the Appendix in case someone asks you a question.

CREATING ENGAGING SLIDES

Now we come to the meat and bone of this chapter. What we have touched upon till now is how to build a good skeleton. Now we come to the core content or the actual cell in the human body.

How do you create a good slide? Honestly, if you can master this art, you will be very very successful in your corporate careers.

Before we understand how to create a good slide, it is important to understand what is a bad slide. Why don't you go through the two images in Figures 9.4 and 9.5, take a couple of minutes and ask yourself what you didn't like about them.

Do not hurry up. It is important to understand what is wrong before we go on to understand what is right about a slide.

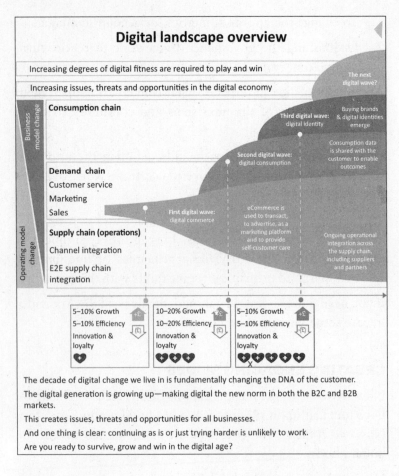

Figure 9.4: What Is Wrong With This Slide? Trust Me, a Lot of Things

No matter how bad you think the slides are, please do not stop reading this book.

When I ask this question at various storytelling workshops, I get a following combination of answers.

I am not sure what is being conveyed.

I couldn't understand the diagram.

The font size was small.

The colours in the diagram made it difficult to read.

The text at the right didn't make sense. It is too long.

Why is there so much white space on the left?

Although I have created this slide for the purpose of showcasing a bad slide, you will be amazed to know that the real-world slides used in corporates are not very different from what is shown here. Let us try a different type of slide. Spend 5 minutes on this one shown in Figure 9.5 and think what is wrong about it.

I get answers along the following lines and I think yours might also be similar,

I don't know what the takeaway is.

It is very difficult to read the diagram.

The text is too dense.

It is so unpleasant to read.

I can't understand what is written in the table to the right.

The font size is too small.

I am getting a headache reading this slide. I need to go to Instagram to view cringeworthy reels!

This slide, like the earlier one, has been created by me as a mock to showcase what is wrong. However, I can assure you enough boardrooms are seeing slides along these lines the world over.

Ask yourself what principle of storytelling is being violated in these slides?

Lack of clear problem statement? Tick.

No Minimalism? Tick.

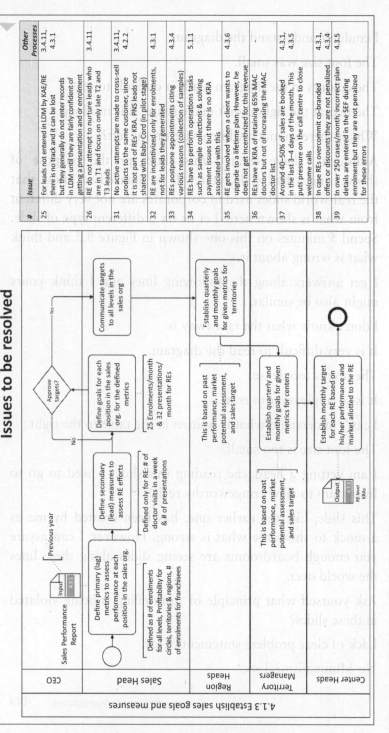

Figure 9.5: What Is Wrong with This Slide? Again, a Lot!

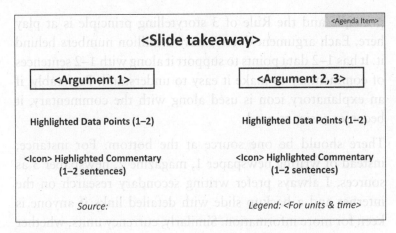

<Agenda Item>

<Slide takeaway>

| <Argument 1> | <Argument 2, 3> |

Highlighted Data Points (1–2)   Highlighted Data Points (1–2)

<Icon> Highlighted Commentary   <Icon> Highlighted Commentary
(1–2 sentences)   (1–2 sentences)

Source: *Legend: <For units & time>*

Figure 9.6: A Recommended Slide Structure for Most of Your Slides

No Rule of 3? Tick.

No power of anecdotes? Tick.

Limited popular culture references? Tick.

Guy Kawasaki's advice on font size? Tick.

Let us move to what should be a good slide structure with a few examples.

Figure 9.6 captures these pain points in a template that you can follow. This is not to suggest that all your slides should be in this format but a majority of your slides where you are presenting an insight or an idea can be.

Why does this slide format work?

It starts with the key takeaway at the top. From our storytelling principle, the problem definition or the impact is clearly mentioned.

To support the insight or the problem, the slide is divided into 2 or 3 parts to support the takeaway. The Minto pyramid principle and the Rule of 3 storytelling principle is at play here. Each argument doesn't have a million numbers behind it. It has 1–2 data points to support it along with 1–2 sentences of commentary to make it easy to understand. Preferably, if an explanatory icon is used along with the commentary, it becomes easier to read.

There should be one source at the bottom. For instance, instead of writing newspaper 1, magazine 2, newspaper 3 as sources, I always prefer writing secondary research on the internet and a backup slide with detailed links if anyone is keen for more information. Similarly, currency units, whether in dollars or euros should be mentioned once at the bottom to clean up space and not use the dollar logo ten times on the slide. Classical minimalism storytelling principle is at play here. You will notice on the top right corner, there is a link to the overall presentation. It will tell you where this slide fits into the overall scheme of things.

I know this is difficult to digest. Let us take a few examples.

Let us start with an example I have created.

In Figure 9.7, the takeaway is clear that e-commerce is likely to rise driven by two key factors. More women will shop online due to convenience and the pandemic and the basket size will increase due to customization of products and greater familiarity.

For each of these arguments, a chart is given with the trend. You will notice units are mentioned once on the axis to avoid clutter. Not too much text with either of these arguments.

Similarly, only the starting and the ending values are mentioned on the x-axis on the chart and not the value in every year is mentioned to maintain a clean look. For instance, on the x-axis, you have 2015 and 2022E (E is estimate) rather than mentioning 2015, 2016, 2017, 2018, 2019, 2020, 2021 and

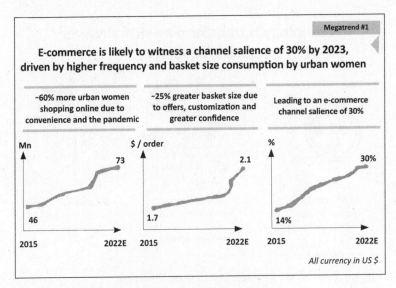

Figure 9.7: What Is Right about This Slide?

Source: Secondary Research, Forbes & Nielsen

2022E. Similarly, only 46 and 73 are shown as the first and the last data points on the leftmost chart to keep a clean chart.

The footnotes are clean. There is just one line for source and a common line for the currency. You will notice on the top right, there is a caption called 'Mega-trend 1', it indicates where this slide stands with regard to the overall document structure. The document might have '5 Mega-trends' to watch out for in the next few years and this slide might be 'Mega-trend 1'.

Let us take another example.

Eric Schmidt, ex-CEO of Google and author of *How Google Works*, along with his co-author Jonathan Rosenberg, shares his lessons on running Google for over a decade. He released a visual preview document for the book, which is widely available on the internet.

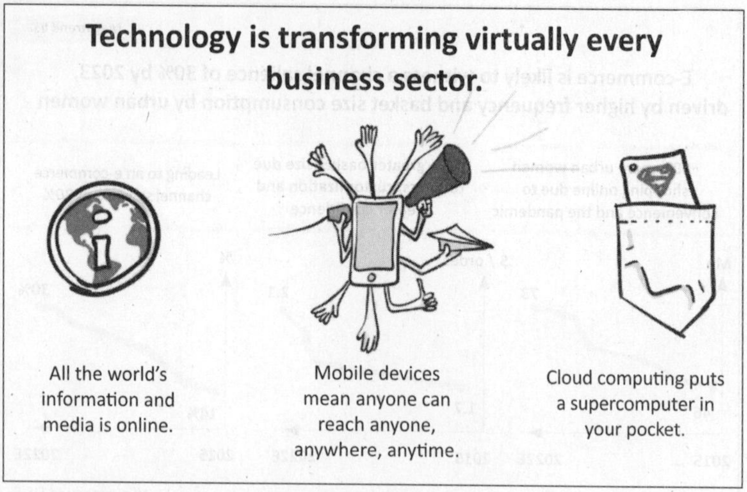

Technology is transforming virtually every business sector.

All the world's information and media is online.

Mobile devices mean anyone can reach anyone, anywhere, anytime.

Cloud computing puts a supercomputer in your pocket.

Figure 9.8: What Is Right with This Slide?

The interesting aspect is there is no voice over for this document but only a set of slides. Let us take a look at a one of them in Figure 9.8.

In this slide, there is a clear message that technology is transforming every sector and by what is it being driven. You will notice 3 sub-arguments. Each sub-argument has a sentence and one image to make the point.

Very simple. Very easy to understand.

Minimalism? Tick.

Rule of 3? Tick.

Clear problem definition or takeaway? Tick.

Great storytelling? Tick.

I would urge you to go through the remaining document too. These storytelling principles are consistent in the remaining slides too.

BUT DO THE BASICS WELL

I want to make something amply clear.

While storytelling using the pyramid principle, minimalistic slide making and rule of 3 are all highly effective, nothing replaces the basics. I have seen basic mistakes in many CEO reviews that have shown people in extremely poor light.

By basics, I mean not checking for spellings, using font sizes that are so small that it is difficult to read them or using old logos of the company on slides.

Mysteriously, one of the most common mistakes I have seen is how presenters get the first slide completely wrong. For instance, on the first slide or the cover slide, the date is often incorrect or the name of the person the meeting is addressed to is incorrect or the company logo is an outdated one or the name of the meeting is incorrect.

Avoid calling a meeting 'Review meeting with the board' when the board members are not sitting in the review and it is only the CEO and the presentation is for his/her consumption.

Avoid writing, 'CEO review 2021' when you are sitting in the year 2022.

Avoid using colours that make it difficult to read. The general principle is to use the approved brand colours of your company. If you have to make a choice, go for contrasts such that the text colour and the background colour are in deep contrast to make it easier to read.

I worked with a senior partner who would get terribly offended if the sentence I wrote went into two lines. He almost felt violated if the sentence in a bullet went into the second line. In hindsight, I do realize that his intentions were good. If a sentence on a slide goes into the second sentence, it disrupts the reading experience. A bullet should hav one line always. If there is another related point, it can be another bullet or a sub-bullet under the main bullet. For someone who is as garrulous as I am, it took me 5 years to master the art. But I can vouch for its efficacy. I am sure you can get there much faster.

To summarize, we have looked at how storytelling can be used to build a great document. In the next few pages, we will look at how storytelling can be used to amplify the engagement with your audience.

UNDERSTAND YOUR AUDIENCE THROUGH SOCIAL STYLES

You can profile your audience using the concept of social styles. Psychologists David Merrill and Roger Reid classified how people like to be engaged in four main buckets—Analyticals, Drivers, Expressives and Amiables.[5] I should start by saying that no style is better than the other. They are all different and have unique nuances about them. I have deployed this technique for over a decade and have found it extremely useful.

Let us spend time on each of the social styles and what you can do with your content to appeal to them.

If you meet someone who doesn't like to do small talk, is always talking to the point, wanting to know the timelines and progress against each activity, highly action- and goal-oriented, does not waste time on intellectual stimulation, can be perceived as blunt or harsh in their language, you are speaking to a 'Driver'.

---

[5] I do not want to provide a specific link for this as there are tons of materials on this on the internet

Clear body cues to identify a 'Driver' include limited small talk, conversations around deadlines for activities, practical discussions, no intellectual hogwash and often a direct or sometimes a harsh way of talking.

For such people, your content should always showcase action orientation, by when will something get done, if something got delayed, why did it get delayed and by when will it get corrected.

In my experience, 'Drivers' are typically chief operating officers (COOs) or Sales Heads at corporations.

If you meet someone who is highly detail oriented, wants to understand the numbers behind every statement of yours, is keen to spend time on the assumptions of your business models, is highly methodical and places a high value on accuracy, you are speaking to an 'Analytical' social style.

Clear cues to identify an 'Analytical' include them repeatedly using numbers in every statement, their capability of attending long meetings without losing attention, being serious in disposition, their love of Excel and curiosity to understand the working behind every estimate. They also usually have very neat and organized desks.

For such people, your content should be data heavy and you should send a pre-read with the workings before a discussion and be willing to shift to an Excel sheet in the meeting to explain your line of reasoning. Also, be prepared for long meetings. Very long ones.

In my experience, 'Analytical' social style people are typically CFOs.

If you meet someone who is sociable, enthusiastic, talks about the future, is passionate, speaks about big ideas, gets along with a lot of people, is an excellent storyteller, you are speaking to an 'Expressive' social style.

Clear cues to identify an 'Expressive' include genuine energy, warmth and belief in what they are saying, their self-belief in trying to shape the future, little tendency to get hands into Excel sheet assumptions, timelines and quick reaction times to any statement you make.

For such people, your content should be highly visual. Use a generous dosage of movie video clips, great quotations, limited text and numbers, sporting metaphors and a narrative about shaping the future.

In my experience, 'Expressive' social style people are generally Chief Marketing Officers (CMOs) or a lot of entrepreneurs serving end consumers like you and me.

If you meet someone who is clearly easy to talk to, respectful to everyone in the room, will not try to hog the limelight, concerned about what is happening to their employees or their vendors or their customers, generally agreeable and will not take an extreme stand, you are speaking to an 'Amiable'.

Clear cues to identify an 'Amiable' are an easy speaking style, zero interruption when someone else is speaking, a huge amount of patience and a general sense of being respectful and polite with everyone. They may or may not be into numbers and their underlying assumptions.

For such people, you should always talk about impact on human beings first—consumers, vendors, employees, etc. If making a business case, you should highlight how the lives of such people will change positively once you undertake that initiative.

In my experience, 'Amiable' social style people are generally Human Resources (HR) Heads or CEOs of companies that have a very intelligent talent pool.

Now, let us go through some tricky questions.

Can one person show multiple styles? Absolutely, they can. In all likelihood, every person will show traits of all four social styles. However, most people have one dominant style that you should cater to.

So what happens if people with different social styles are together in a room? If you do not get time to cater to them individually earlier on, you should ideally cater to the most important person in the room. Common sense, isn't it?

How do you handle a problem creator? In any discussion, there are people who always try to poke holes in what you are saying and attempt to make you look bad. Ideally, you should align them before the meeting in case their voice matters in that discussion. In case you are not able to align them, you should avoid taking questions till a majority of your messages have been landed. This will ensure that either some of your messages might answer the problem creator's potential question or that the remaining audience gets all your messages without getting stuck in the problem creator's narrative.

Some of you may be curious on my social style. Aren't you? I am sure you are.

Let me narrate this interesting anecdote to you. I always believed I was an 'Analytical' social style. However, I used to ask my team on what they thought my social style was. Their answers were often either 'Expressive' or 'Amiable'. This has been my team's consistent view over the last many years.

Over a period of time, I have come to the conclusion I am likely to be an 'Expressive'. Partially explains why I have written a book on storytelling.

What is your social style?

You might also be curious on what the social styles of famous people are. So here is my take on social styles of famous people. Elon Musk, a revolutionary business person, is a likely 'Expressive'. So in my view is ex-President of the United States of America, Barack Obama. Virat Kohli, a great Indian cricketer, is likely to be a 'Driver'. So in my view is Hollywood actress Priyanka Chopra. Roger Federer, a champion tennis player, is likely to be 'Amiable'. So in my view is American philanthropist Melinda Gates. Tim Cook, CEO of Apple, is likely to be an 'Analytical'. So in my view is Mukesh Ambani, one of the richest business persons from India.

LEVERAGE THE POWER OF QUOTES

Some of you may be intrigued on how quotes can be influential while presenting. Let me give you a few examples.

One of the greatest sporting icons of all time and legendary basketball player, Michael Jordan, had retired at the peak of his career in 1993 after the tragic death of his father along with tremendous fatigue. When he decided to come out of retirement in 1995, he asked his agent David Falk to write a couple of versions of the news release. Jordan somehow didn't like the options and said he would do it himself. In one of the most iconic quotes of all time, he sent across a fax that said, 'I'm back.'

And nothing else. This quote has been used by business leaders across numerous situations citing the return of the previous founder or in a reference to the good old days.

For people curious about how Jordan's career went after that, the Chicago Bulls won the National Basketball Association (NBA) championships in 1996, 1997 and 1998 cementing him as one of the, if not THE, greatest of all time.

When Indian Prime Minister Narendra Modi wanted to flag off a movement, the Swachh Bharat Abhiyan, or Clean India Movement in 2014, he quoted Mahatma Gandhi to introduce the idea,

'Mahatma Gandhi never compromised on cleanliness. He gave us freedom. We should give him a clean India.'

The movement and the quote went on to capture the imagination of millions of Indians as they undertook upon themselves to keep their own surroundings clean.

Sheryl Sandberg, ex-COO of Meta, ex-Facebook, has a plethora of quotes from her book *Lean In: Women, Work and the Will to Lead* that are used across different occasions. I have seen the following one used across Indian business houses when they are trying to promote women leadership to the highest echelons of power.

'In the future, there will be no female leaders. There will just be leaders.'

So do quotes work? Undoubtedly. They are an extremely powerful storytelling tool

How do they work? They help you introduce complex ideas or challenge your thinking or make a big announcement as the three examples earlier show.

But why do quotes work? This is a very interesting question and has to go back to how your brain operates.

In the TEDx talk on 'The Power of Quotes' by Alex Sheen, he suggests that quotes are a great way to introduce new ideas and introduce a perspective to serve a greater purpose. In his speech, he takes a collection of 18 random quotes and starts repeating them one after another. Mysteriously, they start making sense in a weird way. Let me give you a short sample from his speech,

> As I grow older, I realise that the few joys of childhood are the best that lives have to give. But the best way to not feel hopeless is to get out there and do something. Don't wait for good things to happen to you. If you go out there, you make good things happen, you fill the world with hope.

These three quotes are completely unrelated but somehow when you put them together, you can get your brain to form a story in your mind.

And that is exactly why quotes work. They follow the basic rules of storytelling.

They are minimalistic.

They appeal to your brain because they stimulate it and your brain can visualize an alternate environment where that quote might be applicable.

Your brain tries to form a pattern in its mind.

Quotes helps bring many people under a common roof, just like the concept of a corporation or a football club does or popular culture does.

So go ahead and use quotes as an extremely powerful story-telling tool when you want to challenge thinking, introduce a complicated idea or just bring many people under a common roof.

There are many other ways storytelling can be used with written documents to drive impact.

It can be used to drive controversial messages.

It can be used to scare the CEO.

It can be used to deliver bad news.

How can the power of colours be used effectively?

How can symbols be used to drive powerful messages?

How can you use humour as a storytelling tool?

We will read about these applications in the subsequent chapter. My hunch is you will love that chapter.

DON'T RANT, BE DIRECT

I have spent 20 plus pages in this chapter on PowerPoint presentations but it is not the most important written document you will work on. In your entire corporate career, presentations will take a lot of your time but there is another written document that will take a much longer part of your life. My guess is it might take 3–4 hours of your daily life even now.

Can you guess what that is? Let me give you a few clues.

Sabeer Bhatia, a very rich technology businessman is associated with it.

A very famous movie is associated with it.

Google revolutionized how we work with it.

It is pretty obvious by now. It is your email.

In case you are wondering how, I am referring to the 1998 romcom movie, *You've Got Mail*. Sabeer Bhatia built Hotmail which he sold to Microsoft for US$400 million and which went on to become the base for Microsoft Outlook. Google and Gmail?

I had the bad habit of writing long emails. It took 30 minutes to craft one and it used to take my team a few hours to read, assimilate and reply to it. Honestly, a complete waste of productivity for everyone.

One of the greatest hacks of storytelling is to use the principle of minimalism while composing an email. It will save you a couple of hours every day and make everyone's lives a little better.

Here is a template you can follow.

Hi <Person>,

The objective of this email is <inform you> <make you take a decision> <need guidance>.

Here is a summary of the situation,

<Problem> (1–2 sentences)

<Complication> (1–2 sentences)

<Resolution options> (1–2 sentences)

Regards,

Me.

The above template is ruthlessly using minimalism, a clear problem definition and the 3-part structure from the world of movies to drive productivity. The first line clearly says what the objective of the email is and what role you are expected to play in it.

The body of the email should not be more than 4–5 single sentences speaking about the problem, the challenge and the options ahead.

I can personally vouch for this method. It saves me time while typing; it saves me time while reading and it is highly productive.

Some of you may ask what if the issue is more nuanced. I do believe everything can be compressed in 4–5 sentences in life. If the world war briefings could be sent on one page, I am sure an email can be 4–5 sentences. If it is still not possible, a short call is the ideal way forward.

This template has a huge advantage as it prevents you from responding when you are angry or emotional. If you are angry or emotional and want to blast away while typing out

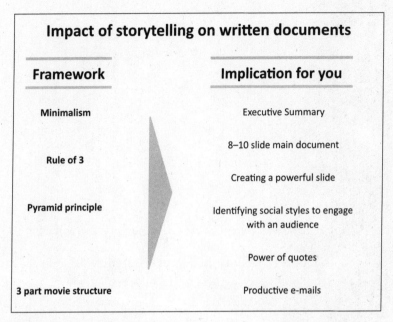

Figure 9.9: Impact of Storytelling on Written Documents

that email, you will in all likelihood write a half page essay. Following such a rigorous template will either force you to get to the point while typing or push it till tomorrow when you have a calmer mind. Both are highly desirable.

Well, with this, we come to the end of this LONG chapter (refer Figure 9.9 for a quick summary). The next chapter is a continuation of how storytelling can bring written documents to life.

Keep your seat belts fastened.

Bad news isn't wine. It doesn't improve with age.

Colin Powell, United States Secretary of
State between 2001 to 2005

*If you have to release bad news
to the public, it would help if you are not ugly.*

Mitch Hedberg, American stand-up comedian

CHAPTER 10

MAKING ELEMENTS STICK

This is one chapter you wouldn't want to give a miss.

In the previous chapter, we looked at using principles of storytelling to create great presentations and effective e-mails. In this chapter, we will explore how you can leverage principles of storytelling to navigate critical situations.

SEMIOTICS... A POWERFUL HIDDEN SCIENCE

Semiotics is an interesting branch of study, which in simple English translates to how signs and symbols create meaning. Any example that comes to your mind? There are plenty.

In its simplest form, it implies chatting with a friend of yours using stickers or emoticons. Each emoticon—a smile, a frown, a hug or a rant conveys a certain meaning. Similarly, traffic lights, red or green, convey a certain meaning. Red means stop and green means proceed. This is what it is supposed to mean irrespective of whether you want to follow it or not. In the washroom, a red coloured tap indicates hot water and a blue coloured tap indicates cold water.

The basic question is, are symbols powerful?

Think of a slightly eaten fruit and if I tell you it is an apple, does it remind you of something?

Think of a red-coloured background with a golden arch in the shape of the letter 'M' arched on it. What does it remind you of?

Four interlocking rings on a silver background. Does it remind you of anything? Let me give you a hint. It is something you aspire for.

Symbols are brought to life by company logos. They become a huge part of the brand experience whether it is Apple, McDonald's or Audi. Notice none of these three logos, as described above, have the company name written on them but once you see the logo, they become obvious in your mind. Not to say logos aren't controversial. In 2014, Airbnb's logo received massive online backlash because it seemed to resemble sexual organs.[1]

How else do you think symbols become powerful?

Let's go to my favourite topic, the world of movies. We also discussed this in Chapter 3, titled, 'How does Hollywood use Storytelling'. In the world of movies, objects often become defining metaphors in a narrative. In that chapter, we discussed the following examples.

Leonardo DiCaprio, in the movie *Inception*, is seen carrying a spinning top with him. If the top keeps spinning, he is still in the dreamworld. If the top stops spinning, it means he is back in the real world. The movie ends on an open note, as we don't know if he comes back to the real world or is still in the dreamworld, as we don't know if the top keeps spinning or stops spinning at the end of the movie.

In Chapter 3, we also looked at the role 'the rock' plays in the movie *Parasite*, where it is supposed to bring prosperity

---

[1] Explanation as to why the Airbnb logo received so much backlash: https://www.bbc.com/news/technology-28343130

to the Kim family but it turns out to be a fake one at the end of the movie putting a full stop to the metaphorical social mobility.

Similarly, in the 2019 blockbuster movie, *Joker*, the clown make-up has hidden meanings throughout the movie. It signifies an aid for entertainment, people living in different societies and eventually represents the rebellion against the ruling elite.

We also covered the role colour and lighting play in Chapter 3. In a TED Talk given by Danielle Feinberg, Director of Photography at Pixar Animation Studios, she speaks about the incredible role lighting and colour play in changing the entire experience of a movie. She speaks of the role of lighting to bring the underwater stories to life in *Finding Nemo*.

Street art, or graffiti, is known to be an extremely powerful medium to express yourself. Its disproportionate impact often has its roots in semiotics. Do you think graffiti works? A simple example about the power of street art or graffiti is that an entire theory has been built to address it called the 'Broken Windows Theory'. The 'Broken Windows Theory', introduced by social scientists James Wilson and George Kelling, claims that regular policing to clean up arts of graffiti can prevent serious crimes in the future. The reason it is called 'Broken Windows' is because when people see an environment that is not in order as characterized by broken windows in a locality, crime tends to be higher. That statement in itself indicates the power of symbols of protest or graffiti on walls. This is the controversial theory that was deployed by the police to clean up crime in New York City in the 1990s.

But why does semiotics or the science of symbols or images or even colours work so well?

The answer is something we touched upon in an earlier chapter on 'Creating Legendary Consumer Brands'.

More than 75 per cent of the decision-making in your brain is controlled by the reptilian (instinctual) and the limbic (emotional) part of your brain. The reptilian part of the brain is related to primitive habits linked to thirst, hunger, everyday habits such as putting your phone for charging and so on. The limbic portion of your brain is involved in behavioural and emotional responses. These two parts of the brain are driven by emotion rather than rationality. These two parts of the brain are why you make irrational decisions while shopping. Semiotics, or its impact through sight and emotion, triggers this part of the brain viciously.

In the next few pages, let us see how you can use symbols, colours and objects to make your narratives stick.

CONVEYING BAD NEWS THROUGH IMAGES AND METAPHORS

One of the toughest jobs, whether in corporate life, in entrepreneurship or with your romantic partner is to convey bad news. While the ability to call a spade a spade looks good when it comes from Harvey Specter in the hit series 'Suits', it rarely does so coming from your and my mouths in real life.

The reasons for this are fairly obvious. No one likes to be told bad things on their face. Trust me, 'shoot the messenger of bad news', is a very real threat.

In certain cultures, like Asian cultures and especially the part of the world I come from, conveying bad news is often seen as tricky business. You risk offending the ego of the other person. You risk being synonymous with the bad news itself and losing your credibility. Due to these risks, sometimes you don't communicate at all, which can be a devastating alternative.

During my 20s, when I was fairly idealistic, I tried to embrace the 'call a spade a spade' tactic and went to the CEO of a fairly large company to say this,

> Your marketing function doesn't understand the modern-day consumer. They don't understand quantitative and qualitative measures of consumer behaviour. They are just copying what the competition is doing. I have 30 plus examples to prove my point if you want to go through it.

The CEO turned out to be the erstwhile head of the marketing function before taking up the role of the CEO. And she saw it as a personal insult. Despite my numerous attempts to make her see the 30 plus examples I had gathered, it faltered badly.

Over a period of time, I have gotten better at delivering bad news. Images and metaphors have helped me immensely.

A CEO of a mid-sized company, who was also the owner of the firm, was keen to undertake a digital transformation programme for his company. His company completely sucked and he wanted to make a few incremental steps. As I began my advisory journey with him, I realized he was suddenly being excessively greedy and was worrying about what could happen 30 years later when he had barely begun to walk. To make him get the point, I used the following sports metaphor,

'If you are learning to pick up the tennis racket in your backyard, maybe you shouldn't worry about playing Roger Federer in a Wimbledon final.'

How would you have reacted to the above metaphor? Read on about how this meeting went. There was pin drop silence. From both sides.

I do consider this one of my braver smart-ass moves. After a very uncomfortable pause of 30 LONG seconds, he did crack into a smile and got the message that he was worrying over things he shouldn't worry about.

To continue the argument, I have found sporting metaphors to be extremely powerful.

If someone is questioning that the leadership is old and all the seniors need to be fired, you may use,

'Please remind me what was the average age of the Chicago Bulls basketball team that won its 6th NBA title under Michael Jordan'.

If someone is suggesting that the leadership team doesn't need any young blood and only experience matters, you may use,

'Please remind me how many big players were playing in the T20 cricket world cup in 2007 when Mahendra Singh Dhoni lifted his first World Cup trophy.'

As a supervisor, which most of us will be at some point, if you find your teammate who has a lot of talent but is slacking at work, you can always use such sporting metaphors to provide feedback without sounding rude while being direct. For instance.

> Two cricketers in their teenage years started playing at the same time. One had flair and grace and was considered the more talented. The other one, while good, was considered less talented. Both started playing cricket for the Indian national team in the late 80s/early 90s. The first one, due to his grace and talent had an outstanding start to his career while the second one showed a lot of promise but didn't have as good a start.
>
> After twenty years, the first one, Vinod Kambli was seen as a cricketing failure due to his lack of discipline and addiction to the glamorous life while the second one, Sachin Tendulkar, went on to become the greatest of all time with his tremendous hard work and dedication. Which one do you want to be?

I have personally used this story many times and I have seen it resonate very strongly and have the desired effect. You may use a similar story in case cricket is not the primary sport in your part of the world. When you use sporting metaphors, you have to be relatively certain the other person follows the sport. Using a Tiger Woods metaphor on someone who doesn't understand golf is not the greatest idea.

An equally effective way to pass on very tricky messages is to use cartoon strips or famous memes from the internet. In my experience, this has incredible power to communicate any ugly message you want to drive home.

I once had to present to the C-suite of a moderately large FMCG company and I wanted to convey the message that the company isn't being true to its intent of undertaking a journey towards modernizing itself. And unfortunately, the problem was the group of people whom I was going to present to. They said they wanted to change but were rooted to the outdated old times.

It was always going to be a brave strategy to tell the senior-most leadership in an FMCG company, some of whom were always on the front pages of business newspapers, that you completely suck. And you are stuck in the Stone Age.

I picked this very famous image from social media (Figure 10.1) and put it as the first slide of the presentation 15 minutes before the meeting started. As everyone entered the boardroom, he/she encountered this image as the first slide to be presented. I didn't have to say a word. The message was passed on loud and clear. And I didn't have to utter a word.

Similarly, I was once invited to address the leadership team of one of India's biggest consumer durables companies.

Figure 10.1: Who Says Random Images on Social Media Don't Work? If I Could Convince the Leadership of a Large FMCG Company Using This Image, Who Knows, Your Instagram Reel Might Also Help You in Some Board Meeting

It was a fairly conservative firm when it came to hiring women. Although it did express an intent to hire more women across the board, the everyday psyche and years of conservative upbringing were proving difficult. Here is another famous social media meme that came to the rescue (Figure 10.2).

I recently had to convince a chief human resources officer (CHRO) of a large company that maybe he should drop the bell curve and the excessive importance of performance-related metrics. While I was writing this chapter, *Squid Game* had become a global sensation. I told him, 'The most

"Describe what you can bring to this company."

Figure 10.2: Need I Say More? This is Truly One of the Most Powerful Images to Advocate Gender Inclusion Across the Board

performance-centric culture is *Squid Game* where 450 plus participants are killed in 8 episodes to have 1 deserving winner. There is backstabbing, treachery, foul play, murder and lack of human values. Is that what you want?'

This one didn't quite land, to be honest. He replied that he loved *Squid Game* and real life should mirror that show. I think he was deranged or high.

Another source of pictorial content to convey bad news, which has never failed me, is cartoon strips. For the uninitiated, cartoon strips are not meant for children. They pretend to be produced for children but are actually directed at everyone. And somehow, they can portray the most gruesome societal truth in an entertaining byte-sized format (Figure 10.3).

If you want to get started, try Calvin and Hobbes, Garfield or even Dennis the Menace.

Figure 10.3: When You Have to Tell Your Overexcited Entrepreneur Friend That His Products Might Not Sell Like the First iPhone![2]

Some of you pessimists might ask me when does this technique not work. Well, there are quite a few scenarios. Never pick up a metaphor from a religious text—the Bhagavad Gita, the Quran, the Holy Bible or the Batman comic strip. I am joking about the Batman comic strip. The reason is that nothing divides an audience like a religious text and religious texts are becoming more complicated as the years go by. A historical villain might no longer be the villain but turn out to be a sympathetic anti-hero. I am not going to give a religious example here to prove my point and ruin this mega bestselling book by getting it burned on every other street.

But for the nerds who love superheroes, Joker was always the villain and Batman the hero. Do you still believe that after watching Joaquin Phoenix play the title role in the 2019 blockbuster movie, *Joker*?

---

[2] Source of the cartoon strip is obviously Calvin and Hobbes. But for the internet purists, this is where I got it from, http://bestofcalvinandhobbes. com/2011/10/a-swifty-kick-in-the-butt-is-for-sale/

The other scenario where this technique of metaphor-based storytelling doesn't work is if the target in your story is a popular character. In case you want to tell a CEO that he or she is past his/her prime, avoid commenting that Roger Federer is a shadow of himself over the last few years. A die-hard Federer fan, me included, will never forgive you for that.

Another scenario where metaphor-based storytelling might not have the desired effect is when you are asking for a deserved promotion, career growth or a salary hike. In my view, when these kinds of conversations are happening, it is best to get straight to the point rather than using a sporting metaphor. Saying Roger Federer's advertising endorsement rates grew five times once he won his first Wimbledon, and as a result so should yours because you smashed all business metrics somehow doesn't seem right.

COLOURS TO DIRECT YOUR AUDIENCE

I touched earlier upon how colour is an extremely important element to drive your messages. But how do you use colours in a PowerPoint presentation? Let me give you a few examples. Typically, the most important way to use colour is to use it as a background in a slide. It can help set and direct the mood of the audience in the direction you like as shown in Figure 10.4.

The most powerful colour, undoubtedly, is black. In the famous TV game show *Family Feud*, host Steve Harper asks one of his participants, 'Name something that looks good in black.' The participant replies, 'People'. Steve loves the answer and slams the table.[3]

---

[3] The entire episode is equally entertaining: https://www.youtube.com/watch?v=lkFG_2F8ygY

> **Going forward, we will only focus on
> our top 3 businesses.**
>
> **We will divest the remaining over the next 2 years.**
>
> **We will pivot to be digitally oriented and
> grow only with profit.**
>
> **It will not be easy but being a leader never is.**

Figure 10.4: Announcing to a Company About a Tough But Necessary Future Direction

Black, as a background colour, is used to announce powerful transformation, a new way to work, a new motto or a slow but impactful change into the future. It is not coincidental that all transition slides are by default, black. If you are a student of the mystical sciences in Hinduism, the God of slow but permanent transformation, Saturn, is often shown in black.

The safest background colour is white. Even this book is written in the background colour of white. White as a background can accommodate any type of message or any type of slide across any type of audience. However, white can also be boring. I personally think changing the background colour from white to light grey can make a slide extremely aesthetic. I show the same slide with a white background and with a grey background in Figures 10.5 and 10.6. Given the print of this book is in black and white, you might not be able to appreciate the difference. But in the real world, it is a very handy hack.

How do you show optimism in a slide? Say a corporate offsite is coming up and you want to announce it. Or you

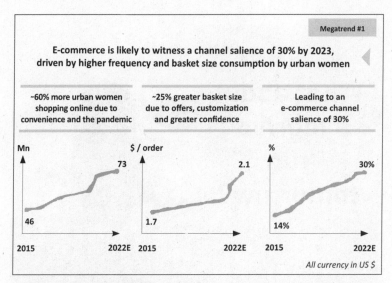

Figure 10.5: A Slide We Discussed in an Earlier Chapter, With a White Background

Source: Secondary Research, Forbes & Nielsen

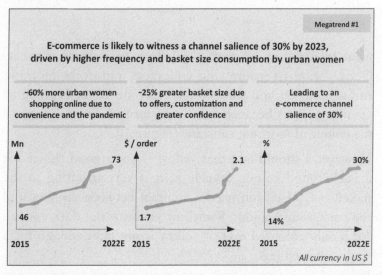

Figure 10.6: The Same Slide with a Grey Background. In the Real World, Grey Looks Better Than a Clean White Background

Source: Secondary Research, Forbes & Nielsen

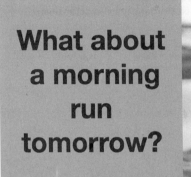
What about a morning run tomorrow?

Figure 10.7: Orange as a Background Conveys Optimism. Plus, the Golden Retriever Adds to the Aesthetic Appeal

want to wake up an audience before an icebreaker event. Or you want to ensure your colleagues join in the morning run session. Or you want to tell everyone he/she is going to get nice goodies because they outperformed. Enter orange or the colour of morning sunshine (Figure 10.7).

However, I should add that yellow is not a good choice for a background colour. Somehow, it is very irritating to the naked eye. Also, you need a contrast between the text and the background colour. Somehow yellow is not dark enough for a light-coloured text or yellow is not light enough for a dark-coloured text.

How do you show passion, energy, focus, drive and results? Enter the Martian colour, red. Red denotes energy, passion, blood and fire. If you want to announce to your team that you are entering the battlefield against your arch-competitor, red is the background colour you are looking for (Figure 10.8). If you want to show blood and touch on taboo topics like women's menstruation, red is your best ally. Although sometimes, red can also show that something is not fine and needs to be focused on.

One of the safer, positivity-oriented colours is green. It represents everything positive, progress in a project or good things happening in general. In financial statements, green is used to indicate metrics where you have done well. Similarly, everything related to the natural world—earth, nature, climate and sustainability—is always shown in green. If you are creating a presentation on the environment and sustainability, green is your principal ally.

Using colour is an extremely powerful way to direct an audience's attention. These colours are not just restricted to PowerPoint slides but can also be used in product brochures, packaging labels of your product or sometimes, even the attire you choose to wear. If you want to land a serious message about a difficult future transformation, wear a three-piece black or navy blue suit. Something more optimistic, go for lighter shades.

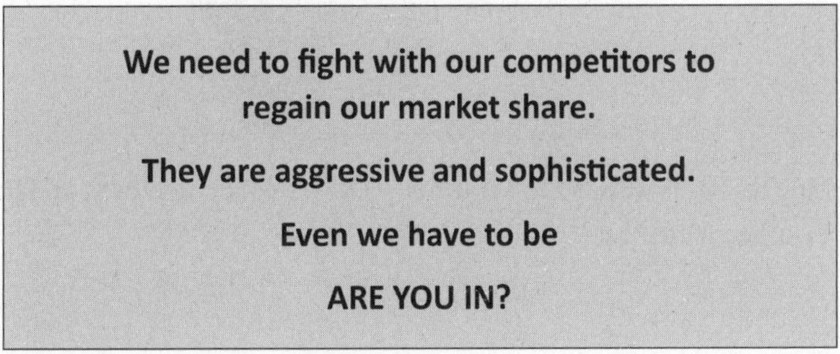

We need to fight with our competitors to regain our market share.

They are aggressive and sophisticated.

Even we have to be

ARE YOU IN?

Figure 10.8: If You Are Giving a Clarion Call to Your Sales Team to Fight, Red is Your Best Ally

SCARE THE CEO

What do you do when your stakeholder, an influential one, is not budging? Your stakeholder can be your CEO, your investor or your immediate boss. As with most things in life, there is a carrot and there is a stick. You always start with a carrot, especially in a large group.

One of the tactics that works with groups of senior leaders in an attempt to nudge them to think differently is to show them an image with multiple meanings and ask them to spot the first thing they see. For instance, in Figure 10.9, do you see the duck or do you see the rabbit? When I have conducted such an exercise in groups, somehow, half the group sees one image and the other half sees the other image. It is a very powerful way to tell a group that your view isn't necessarily the right view. There is an equally powerful other world view. The leaders appreciate this exercise because it is people like them, as competent as them, who are seeing the other world view in the same room.

Figure 10.9: What Do You See? Do You See a Duck or Do You See a Rabbit?[4]

---

[4] I googled images with dual meanings and picked this one from that. The link from where I got the image is: https://www.opticalillusionsportal. com/50-lovely-multiple-illusions/

Moving on, how do you get a group of senior leaders to shut up and start cooperating in a workshop? One way is to tell them to 'shut up and behave themselves' in the workshop. It might backfire and you might ruffle egos. The other way is to use an old semiotics set of symbols available to humankind—traffic signs.

This is a true story. I was once conducting a leadership workshop for a client that had an abundance of hyperactive alpha male personalities. Clearly, it was going to be difficult for me to control the group. There was hostility in the air as their own environment was hypercompetitive and partially toxic. I wanted to tell them to behave themselves in the workshop and maintain basic decency so that we could go through our agenda and be productive. But with such hyperactive, dominating personalities, it is difficult to say something. They also have extremely strong egos—just like eggshells. Hence, I used the symbols in Figure 10.10.

The traffic signals have powerful messages beneath them. 'Horn Prohibited' means do not unnecessarily heckle a fellow participant. 'No Overtaking' means do not turn this workshop into a competition where one person has to win. 'No Vehicles in Both Directions' means be constructive and not critical of others. 'Speed Limit' means be patient and do not hurry to get to the answer. You should give this semiotic storytelling method of using symbols a try. The reptilian and the emotional brain of your participants will love it.

Sometimes, the carrot is good but the stick is essential. Sometimes, you HAVE to tell a senior leader honestly and show them the mirror. According to a study by *Harvard Business Review* titled 'What CEOs are afraid of',[5] the primary fear of

---

[5] Link to the interesting study: https://hbr.org/2015/02/what-ceos-are-afraid-of To be honest, you will know this intuitively

Rules for today's workshop

**HORN
PROHIBITED**

**NO
OVERTAKING**

**NO VEHICLES IN
BOTH DIRECTION**

SPEED LIMIT

Figure 10.10: Using Traffic Signals to Police a Bunch of Hyperactive Senior Leaders

senior leaders is to not look incompetent to everyone or be an underachiever. You can use this very effectively to drive home a message in case someone isn't getting the point.

I was once advising a son of the founder of the company. The son, full of energy and valour, wanted to discount everything that his father had done and only pursue the fashionable cool things. While his intent was good, the old things his father had built were 90 per cent of his business and would remain that for some time. Despite my advising him not to ignore the traditional business, he refused to do so. Finally, I told him one day that I wish him the best of luck but hope his decisions don't make people say he wasn't good enough to run the family business.

How do you think the message landed? BANG! He was taken aback by what I told him. He took it in the right spirit because of the inherent respect he had for me. But I had played into a deep psychological problem all leaders have, 'are they good enough to hold that position of power'. He did sober down after that conversation. Although I would recommend such a method of conversation only as a last resort. The last thing you want is for the senior leader to boycott you. Before we move on, give a quick glance to Figure 10.11

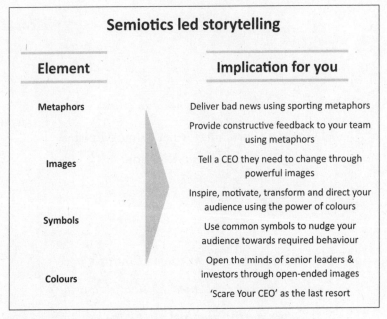

Figure 10.11: Power of Semiotics-led Storytelling

A joke is a very serious thing.

Winston Churchill, former Prime Minister
of the United Kingdom

*You know you have reached middle age
when you are cautioned to slow down by
your doctor, instead of the police.*

Joan Rivers, American actor

CHAPTER 11

LEVERAGING HUMOUR

Being funny is not funny.

If you have to be a master storyteller and a great orator, you have to be good at using humour. Not WhatsApp forwards or Instagram memes but you have to genuinely possess a witty sense of humour. It helps you build audience traction, may land you that dream date and even make you popular in your social circles.

But before we move forward, what is humour? When I was writing this chapter, I was very curious about the definition of humour. Surely, some smart intellectual must have researched the definition of humour. Turns out someone has.

In a TEDx talk given by Peter McGraw on 'What Makes Things Funny', he describes a theoretical construct behind humour, the 'Benign Violation theory'.[1] For something to be funny, there needs to be a violation that is essentially something that threatens or is outside your belief system. That violation has to be benign so that there is no actual danger involved. For instance, kids being tickled keep laughing because there is a violation as you are entering their private space but it is benign because they know you won't hurt them. When

---

[1] Is it funny that someone did research on being funny? https://humorresearchlab.com/benign-violation-theory/

you look at a cartoon series like *Tom and Jerry*, they keep attacking each other, which is a violation, but you know it is benign as it is in good jest and it is a cartoon series. No one is actually getting hurt.

When the situation doesn't seem benign humour turns offensive—a personal insult, a physical prank the other person doesn't appreciate or something deeply offensive to a group of people. When such situations happen, Will Smith walks up on stage and lets Chris Rock know what he thinks of his sense of humour. For some of you who follow award shows like the Golden Globe Awards, you might wonder how Ricky Gervais, despite all his personal jokes over the years has never got into trouble. I would suggest you see videos of his hosting and come to a hypothesis.

My personal view is that his violations are largely benign as they are agreed upon in advance with his close friends (e.g., Steve Carell, the person who plays Michael Scott in *The Office*) and they never make fun of your physical looks nor are deeply personal. He generally jokes around actors being drunk, everyone in Hollywood being a hypocrite and seeking cosmetic surgery.

Or maybe the real explanation is he has just got lucky.

So why does humour work? The answer is obvious.

In a TEDx talk given by Andrew Tarvin on 'Humour that works', he quotes research by *Psychology Today*, American Physiological Society, *Harvard Business Review*, *Journal of Aging Research* that people who use humour at work are more productive, less stressed, paid more and in general happier.

Most of you intuitively know this. But the question again is why?

As you might have guessed by now, most reactions in life are chemically oriented. With humour and when it is well received, it releases endorphins that reduce stress, increase a sense of well-being, reduce pain and increase a sense of pleasure. This is why you see the incredible rise of laughter clubs where people forcibly laugh without a joke to trigger these endorphins. Trust me, this works. You should give it a try.

One of the richest Hollywood actors is actually the funny guy Jerry Seinfeld, of the hit comedy series *Seinfeld*, with an estimated net worth of nearly a billion dollars. Humour sells without any doubt on the big screen, on the small screen, in the corporate boardroom, in brand advertising, with an investor or with your fancy date.

In case you suck at humour, not that I am great at it, this chapter may be for you. In case you are great at humour, this chapter is definitely for you.

LEARN FROM THE BEST

I genuinely think if you have to learn about being funny, you have to watch the stand-up comedians. I don't mean the cringeworthy type that focuses on objectifying women, making racial jokes or picking on members of their audience and hurling insults at them. These tricks are honestly not funny at all, as these violations are far from benign and very dangerous.

I am referring to situations where the stand-up comedian knows he or she cannot be cheap or cringeworthy and has to be genuinely funny. The occasion that fits this narrative is the White House Correspondents' Dinner that is held every year in Washington D.C., capital of the United States. This occasion is attended by the president of the United States, other politicians and members of the press. Over the last few decades, brilliant comedians have been called to roast the American president and members of the press.

On a forum like this, you cannot be cringeworthy as the whole world is watching you including the most powerful politicians of the United States and the media. I would urge you to watch the videos of stand-up comics over the last few years as they roast the American president and members of the press. You might not get some of the local cultural references but it is an excellent learning experience.

I particularly loved the 2022 White House Correspondents' Dinner attended by President Joe Biden, where comedian Trevor Noah performed for everyone. If you carefully analyse the way his and other stand-up comics' jokes work, there are a few principles the comedians regularly follow, as we will discuss in the next few paragraphs.

Remember the 'Rule of 3' where communication is most impactful when things are said in groups of 3 as it is easy for your brain to follow a pattern. Also, remember the 'peak-end theory' where your brain remembers an experience by the ending and how the world of movies has tapped into this philosophy by going for a twist at the end of a movie. Watch both these principles come to life. Trevor Noah landed the following jokes in his 2022 performance.

'President Biden has led the country through some really dark times—the COVID pandemic, the war on Ukraine, the launch of CNN plus.'

The audience erupts into laughter as he sarcastically comments on the failure of CNN Plus—a streaming service where news agency CNN spent nearly 300 million dollars and had to shut it down immediately, less than a month after it was launched.

'Ever since you have come into office, President Biden, things are really looking up. Gas is up. Rent is up. Food is up.'

The president bursts into laughter as Trevor initially tries to praise the president but ends up satirically speaking about the highest inflation the United States is going through in a long time.

Do notice how these jokes are constructed with three phrases and the third being the twist. This is classical storytelling on display with the 'Rule of 3' and the 'peak-end theory' with a twist.

Moment marketing is an excellent tool to build humour in. You will recall from Chapter 7 titled 'Creating Legendary Consumer Brands' that brands are latching onto current affairs and wittily commenting on them to drive humour. In that chapter, we looked at how Indian dairy giant, Amul, brilliantly runs its moment marketing campaigns.

Stand-up comics aren't far behind.

'Thank you President Joe Biden and the First Lady. It is my great honour to be speaking at the nation's most distinguished super-spreader event.'

Trevor makes a reference to how such a large gathering where no one is wearing a mask is likely to spread the virus. He goes on,

'My name is Trevor Noah. You could have picked any comedian, anyone, but you went with the South African variant, very on theme.'

Trevor Noah is from South Africa but the reference here is to the COVID variant from South Africa.

In a later chapter, you will come across a theory called the 'Nested Anecdote' way to construct a personal speech where you start with an anecdote and end with one for massive impact. When you combine this with the 'peak-end theory' with a twist at the end, you get the hilarious performance by former President Barack Obama at the White House Correspondents' Dinner 2015.

During his speech, Obama brings in an anger translator, played by comedian, Keegan Michael-Key, to really say what he wants to say. Obama says the politically correct stuff while his anger translator says the politically incorrect stuff. The twist at the end is when Obama gets angry and his anger translator, ironically, calms him down. Before leaving the stage, his anger translator, tells Obama,

'You don't need an anger translator. You need counselling.'

HUMOUR TO DRIVE STICKINESS

Brands and advertising have historically used humour extremely well to drive stickiness in their campaigns. Let me give you a few examples in my view.

A decade ago, Toyota launched an ad campaign for its Corolla set of cars. A pretty lady is standing by a Toyota Corolla that has broken down by the road. As another car with two young men approaches her, she seductively walks towards them. As the young men decide to slow down to speak to the seductively attractive woman, they suddenly speed away and one man says, 'It is a trap. Have you ever seen a Corolla broken down?' As their car speeds away, the pretty lady is seen turning into a male villain. The ad has nearly 4.5 million views on YouTube with the tagline, 'Toyota Corolla: It's a quality thing'. This is the most common male fantasy almost coming true with an interesting twist at the end. All expressed within 30 seconds. The storytelling principle at play is a popular culture reference of an ultimate male fantasy and peak-end theory with a twist at the end.

I love the 'Hari Sadu' ad by Naukri.com. In that ad, a tyrant of a boss is yelling at his team members. Meanwhile, his secretary steps in and asks him to speak to the restaurant reservation desk where the tyrant boss intends to go in the evening. The person at the reservation desk asks for the tyrant boss' name and he gruffly replies 'Hari Sadu', which the reservation person doesn't catch on. One of his team members, whom he was yelling at, decides to step in to help his boss. He starts spelling out his boss's name, 'Write down Hari Sadu - H for Hitler, A for Arrogant, R for Rascal, I for Idiot'. The ad ends with the tagline, 'Guess who has just heard from us' and you see 'Naukri.com' with the tagline - India's number 1 job site. The storytelling principle at play is the popular culture reference to a tyrant boss and how you humorously deal with them.

One of the most loved ad series is the 'Men will be Men' ads by Seagram's Imperial Blue Music CDs. The ad series humorously plays along the 'perceived' common traits of men as they deal with women in their day-to-day lives. In one of their ads, a pretty lady enters a flight and she requests a man to take the painful middle seat. The man readily agrees to take the painful middle seat due to the prospect of sitting next to the pretty lady. His joy is short-lived as she makes her grandfather sit in the seat and she goes away.

In another ad, a pretty doctor comes to inspect an unconscious man who has his wife sitting next to him. As the pretty doctor feels his pulse, the heart rate of the unconscious man shoots up viciously and recedes when the pretty doctor goes away much to the irritation of his wife. The series appeals to people as it plays to the popular culture reference of 'Men will be Men'. It violates an accepted notion of how men should behave but is seen as largely harmless.

So why do advertisements use humour?

Three-fourths of consumers believe advertisements are more intrusive than ever before.[2]

The same survey indicates that 1 out of 2 consumers find advertisements irritating or not relevant and hence consider blocking them.

I am sure the above metrics are not a surprise to you. Hence, it is no surprise that brands are leveraging humour to release the right chemicals so that their stories stick. The basic principle is to stand out amid the noise without coming across as clingy. Needless to say, when an ad is made, the principle of minimalism in storytelling is automatically factored in as ads are generally between 30 to 60 seconds in length.

BEING FUNNY AT WORK

It is not easy being a funny guy. When I worked in management consulting, one of the partners I worked with must have realized the importance of humour while speaking and tried to get funny while making presentations. He seemed desperate to sound funny to an audience. The anecdotes below are absolutely true.

In case you are that partner who is reading this, well sorry boss, it is high time you get the message. Some of his famous attempted jokes in corporate boardrooms are,

'Knock knock!

Who's there?

Bull.

Bull who?

Bullshitter!'

---

[2] In a survey of US internet consumers by Kantar Millward Brown, 71 per cent of respondents said that ads are more intrusive now than they were three years ago.

The above joke is an attempt to play on the stereotype that management consultants bullshit their way through. Eww! Ewww!

Another one,

'I tried to give feedback to my wife today morning over breakfast. Now I make breakfast.'

Gender stereotypes in the modern-day world rarely work. The reason this doesn't work is because the violation is not benign. This statement is reinforcing an age-old stereotype.

On both these occasions, there was an awkward silence from the leadership teams of the client. I happened to be in both of these meetings. You could pierce the air during that awkward silence.

To say the above joke attempts are cringeworthy is being excessively polite. It is never easy trying to be the funny guy without making a fool of yourself. The last thing you want to appear is a wannabe clown in a very serious forum.

So what is a good sense of humour?

In 2015, the Prime Minister of India, Narendra Modi, went to the United States to address the Indian diaspora. During this time, he was under fierce criticism from the opposition that his budget lacked a sense of long-term vision. While he was addressing this massive gathering, he himself mentioned this criticism and replied to it by saying,

'People are asking me for a vision for the budget. I hope people realize I have come this far in life by selling cups of tea at railway stations.'

The comment was a reference to his humble background and his remarkable success story from being someone who used to sell tea at the roadside to becoming the prime minister of the world's largest democracy. The massive diaspora rose to a standing ovation out of respect and bore a wide chuckle. The opposition rarely raised the point again. The principle of storytelling that is at play is from Chapter 3 titled 'How Does Hollywood Use Storytelling'—a clear problem definition of making an incredible journey from rags-to-riches. This incredible narrative also generates oxytocin, the empathy chemical in your brain.

Hollywood megastar, Brad Pitt, in his acceptance speech at the 26th Annual Screen Actors Guild Awards for his movie *Once Upon a Time in Hollywood*, said,

'Let's be honest, it was a difficult part. Guy who gets high, takes his shirt off, and doesn't get on with his wife? It was a big stretch.'[3]

It was a light-hearted dig at his real-life character playing his reel-life character with his ex-wife Jennifer Anniston cheering him along. This is clearly a violation of his own accepted norm but is largely benign.

In the case of corporate presentations, a sense of humour can be a great weapon or can be a huge source of embarrassment. One of the easiest ways to use humour effectively is to use cartoon strips (e.g., Garfield, Calvin and Hobbes) on slides while providing commentary on them.

A CXO of a Fortune 500 company I was privileged to work with once started the Monday morning review discussion with the strip in Figure 11.1. A tense atmosphere on the eve of the leadership review immediately changed to a room filled with light chuckles. I am not going to name him but I always thought he had an outstanding sense of humour and had he not been a successful CXO, he would have been a very successful stand-up comedian.

---

[3] For the full speech which is highly entertaining, you can refer https://www.vogue.com/article/brad-pitt-funny-sag-awards-acceptance-speech

Figure 11.1: Get Up, It's Monday Morning! Time To Rise and Shine![4]

As the above anecdotes indicate, the golden rule of humour is to laugh at yourself, although in a controlled manner. Making fun of your poor toilet hygiene or how you are an unprofessional worker or how you are a sexual pervert is never a good idea in front of a corporate audience. The reason these don't work is because the violations are not benign. They are serious. However, light-hearted self-deprecating humour is always appreciated.

Following are some of the samples I have always used.

When I wanted to comment that someone's user interface design is downright ugly, I would use,

'I am aesthetically challenged and not the right person to comment on this. But my aesthetically challenged brain suggests that maybe you can relook at…a….b….c….'

To warm up to a stiff audience, making fun of your seemingly old age can lead to a few chuckles and lead people to have a less stiffer bottom side.

'It is high time people like me start accepting we are ageing middle-aged men rather than college students.'

---

[4] For more such hilarious strips, you can visit https://garfieldreviews. wordpress.com/author/icelandicwaffles/

In case you are someone who is strongly opinionated but believes your voice can help steer the discussion in the right direction, referring to your gregariousness can often make you sound less of a virus in a large audience. You could try,

'As you would have figured out by now, I am someone who is in love with his own voice. I wouldn't want to irritate you any further but here is a summary of what I have said till now.'

In case you are succeeding at your workplace and you want to avoid peers getting unnecessarily envious of you, you could try playing the narcissistic card. Some argue you should be more humble if you are doing really well but sometimes people can take it for artificial humility and get more envious. Instead, calling yourself a narcissist, if done correctly, can ease off unnecessary peer gaze. For instance,

'I am on social media 24 × 7. It is an excellent vehicle to serve my narcissistic self.'

Another great vehicle when you are trying to attract an audience's attention is using famous movie lines. In case, you are trying to cheer up a teammate who has lost a business deal,

'My mama always said life was like a box of chocolates. You never know what you're gonna get.' (From *Forrest Gump*, the famous Tom Hanks movie, 1994)

In case you are trying to tell members of an audience that something is not working or a huge crisis is imminent,

'Houston, we have a problem.' (From *Apollo 13*, 1995)

If your colleagues or investors are asking you why you are so interested in tracking your competitors and maybe you should forget them for a while,

'Keep your friends close, but your enemies closer.' (From *The Godfather Part II*, 1974)

Notice the principles of storytelling at play here. There are hordes of popular culture references and minimalism with the above lines. Besides, the violations are all benign. The basic principle of good humour.

There are many small things you can do to make work 'fun'. At a team meeting, you could request every teammate to come up with 3 statements about them, 2 of them that are true and 1 that is not. Everyone else has to guess which statement is not the correct statement. Let me try these 3 statements about myself with you.

Statement 1: I love to get up at 5 AM on a Sunday morning

Statement 2: Once upon a time, I ate half a kilogram cake all by myself at one go

Statement 3: I love to go sky diving.

Which is the incorrect statement? Take a guess.[5]

When you introduce yourself to anyone at work, you could add one line, a quirk about yourself. I often speak about how I am a social media addict at the end of my introduction.

In the TEDx talk by Andrew Narvin on 'Humour at Work', he speaks about how he named the project he was managing 'Project Awesomization' and it resonated a lot with this team.

BEING FUNNY IS SERIOUS BUSINESS

Humour can go horribly wrong if the target is someone else. Once I had a hypothesis, that a lot of us working in corporate and entrepreneurial roles had a toxic sense of humour. By toxic I mean, a sense of humour that gains by laughing at someone else's misery to entertain a crowd. In technical terms, the violation is not benign but highly objectionable. To assess if this hypothesis was true, I put up a post on my LinkedIn page and awaited the social reactions (refer Figure 11.2).

---

[5] Reach out to me on social media and I will let you know one on one.

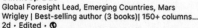

Sandeep Das
Global Foresight Lead, Emerging Countries, Mars Wrigley | Best-selling author (3 books)| 150+ columns...
2d · Edited · ⊙

In an attempt to being funny, a lot of people in corporate India try to put other people down. Sense of humour unfortunately is not a zero sum game. The only way to make people laugh is not by poking fun at somebody else. Here are some basic guidelines everyone should follow (please add if I have missed),

- Avoid hinting that a lady got promoted because she slept with her boss. This is wrong at so many levels.
- Avoiding laughing at a person's height - comments like shortie etc are never taken in a good way
- Avoid laughing at other physical features - lack of hair or an appearing belly!
- Avoid laughing at a childless couple hinting at their lack of manhood or female hood. You might have no idea of the hell they are probably going through.
- Avoid trying to making fun of someone's career or industry just because you don't understand it
- Avoid making fun of someone's low salary - money is often deeply personal
- Avoid making fun of someone's accent especially if they don't come from urban India
- Avoid making fun about the othe person's possible death or diseases. It is absolutely unacceptable!

You don't need to be funny at all. Especially if you think the only way to be funny is by bringing someone down.

The golden rule - if you want to be funny, make fun of yourself as much as you want. It shows security, maturity and a good sense of humour.

Figure 11.2: Is the Above Brand of Humour Reflective of Your Style?

As you can see, I highly underestimated the extent of the toxic sense of humour that has prevailed in our professional lives. The post was viewed nearly 25,000 times in less than 48 hours and went viral after that. It does give you a sense that a lot of people don't have a sense of what is funny and what isn't.

The golden rule, as mentioned in Figure 11.2, is if you want to be funny, make fun of yourself as much as you want. It shows a sense of security, maturity and sometimes a good sense of humour. When you make fun of yourself, you will tend to be classy too. If the violation is on someone else, be absolutely sure it is benign or far away from them.

I also advocate that you stay off holy cows, no pun intended, in our society — avoid any seemingly funny reference to religion and politics. If you recall from an earlier chapter on the evolutionary perspective on storytelling, religion and politics are two of the major stories that have led to the success of the human species. Any reference to these is not only considered offensive but actually seems to introduce friction in the evolutionary brain.

Having a great sense of humour is an excellent tactic for storytelling. Contrary to common belief, people are not born funny. Some develop the skill over a period of time. Including me.

Before you go on to the next chapter, why don't you go laugh at the incompetence of your boss. Now, that is not supposed to be funny. Neither is the illustrative below (Figure 11.3).

Leveraging humour while storytelling	
Storytelling principle	Storytelling principles used in corporate circles
Power of anecdotes	Cartoon strips
Popular culture references	Famous movie lines
Twist at the end	Program names, 2 truths and a lie, quirks while introducing yourself
Minimalism	Moment marketing on current affairs
Rule of 3	Avoid holy cows

Figure 11.3: Leveraging Humour while Storytelling

First get rich, then become a philosopher.

Shah Rukh Khan, one of the world's biggest actors

Looking at all the wonderful faces
here reminds me of the great work that has
been done this year ... by cosmetic surgeons.

Ricky Gervais, while hosting the Golden Globe Awards

CHAPTER 12

BECOMING A MASTER ORATOR

'On the way over here, I made a list of all the people who deserve to be thanked for this award. The list came to 172 names. I obviously can't thank all 172 names so I wrote down the 172 names on individual pieces of paper and they are now in my left hand trouser pocket. I am just going to pick out 3 at random. And everyone else can just lump it.' To the mirth of his audience, he then started picking out three random names from his pocket. The audience erupted as he thanked the name on the first chit—his script supervisor. He then thanked the hair stylist as part of the second chit. He picked out a third chit and threw it away indicating he didn't want to thank that person. When he picked the next chit, he said, 'I would like to thank my agent', took a pause and wittily remarked, 'That is not my handwriting'. Hugh Laurie, the person who played the brilliant but eccentric doctor in House gave one of the wittiest award acceptance speeches when he got the award for Best Actor in a TV Series Drama at the Golden Globe Awards in 2006.

The best orators in life are actually movie stars, stand up-comedians and politicians. And some businesspeople. Only some. In this chapter, we will touch upon how you can become a brilliant orator using the principles of storytelling we have been discussing throughout this book. I should highlight that this topic of being an expert orator has been beaten to death over many decades and hence I will only stick to the storytelling angle of it. Also, this is one of those chapters where you will see interesting nuances from multiple chapters flow in effortlessly. After all, most people think of storytelling as being synonymous with being a great orator.

To be honest, this is one of the easier chapters I have written. But this is probably the most difficult chapter to implement in real life. And hence, I will write largely from my own experience throughout this chapter so that you get a real-world flavour of the challenges and the tricks I have painfully learnt along the way. Not to say I am a great orator but I am definitely better than what I was a few years ago.

Read on.

START AND END WITH AN ANECDOTE

The start of your speech is often the most important part of your speaking experience. You hook your audience in early; they will enjoy and be involved in the experience with you. You lose them in the first 15 seconds; it is largely downhill from there.

Conor Neill, entrepreneur and a professor in leadership communication, in a speech, describes how people typically start a speech.[1] According to him, the following are the templates people generally use,

'Hi, my name is Sandeep Das. I do this role at this company. My speech will talk about this boring topic.' In his view, most people use this kind of an introduction and most of your audience is already losing interest.

---

[1] Here is the link to the YouTube video from his channel: https://www.youtube.com/watch?v=w82a1FT5o88

The other template is,

'Hello, hello. Can you hear me? Is my slide visible? Is my mic working? Am I visible?' Blah!

I can resonate with this template so much. Especially during virtual calls. Or the other template is and I am going to take a very disturbing topic, 'the impact of the pandemic on mental health', to highlight my point,

'Did you know that India lost more people to suicides than to COVID in the year 2020?'[2]

The above three templates are the most common ways to start a speech. However, they are not the most effective. An interesting fact approach still works but isn't as powerful as an anecdote. Let us take the 'fact led way' to start the speech.

'Did you know that India lost more people to suicides than to COVID in the year 2020?'

Or,

'Did you know that India witnessed over 150,000 suicides in 2020, the highest in ten years?'

Or,

'My friend, Dev, used to beat me at tennis every weekend. Then COVID came. And I can't beat him anymore. He committed suicide as the pandemic took a heavy toll on his mental health.'

Which one had the most impact in your view? In all likelihood, you might feel strongly immersed with the third one, even if it is a very disturbing one. The anecdote always works best in hooking your crowd into what you are saying. The anecdote

---

[2] This is a shocking fact: https://www.news18.com/news/india/india-lost-more-people-to-suicide-than-coronavirus-in-2020-shows-ncrb-data-4388651.html

need not be a sad one as it is in this case. The principle of storytelling at play here is that anecdotes always work better than numbers for your brain.

What other types of anecdotes can you start with? If you are an entrepreneur, you can start with your 'Origin Story' on why you started your company. If you recall, we touched upon the 'Origin Story' in Chapter 6 titled 'Becoming a Visionary Entrepreneur'. If you are talking about transforming your company, highlight a successful anecdote of someone's life that has improved significantly as a result of the transformation programme. If you recall, we touched upon the need to create anecdotal success stories in Chapter 5 titled 'Driving Change'. You can also start your speech with a line you want your audience to remember or takeaway or a rallying cry you want to spread.

For instance, the Prime Minister of India, Narendra Modi, starts his speeches with, 'Bharat Mata ki Jai', translating to 'Victory for Mother India'. He has often tried to instil a sense of pride among Indians and 'Bharat Mata ki Jai' is his rallying cry. You can also start with a funny anecdote as some speakers do in their TED speeches. In Chapter 11 titled 'Leveraging Humour', we discussed how you could be genuinely funny without being offensive.

But the anecdote at the beginning cannot be just left loose. It has to be closed appropriately at the end. In computer science programming, there is a principle called nesting where smaller objects are placed inside larger objects and you always close a loop that you open. This principle is equivalent to a toy that children play with, the Russian dolls, which fit within each other and you have to close the biggest doll once you have put everything else in it.

The anecdotes you start with ideally should be closed. If I had to close the anecdote on my friend Dev, I would probably use,

Look to your left or look to your right. One of them is likely battling a serious mental health crisis. My request to you is to reach out to your friends and family members and just ask them if they are okay. A small 'how are you' can go a long way in saving a life.

LEVERAGE POPULAR CULTURE REFERENCES

I am sure you don't want me to tell you, again, that popular culture references—movies and sporting references work with people. You are probably bored by now with me telling you that they capture your audience's brain because they are powerful anecdotes and they are available in common knowledge so everyone gets hooked on them.

I will give you three examples that I have deployed or seen very good speakers do in their careers.

I once watched a head of sales, answer brutal questions from his team about their competitor playing dirty and hence they needed to play dirty too. The head of sales answered the question by playing a video of the following lines that Sylvester Stallone used to address his son who was struggling to make his life a success in the 2006 movie, *Rocky Balboa*.

Let me tell you something you already know. The world ain't all sunshine and rainbows. It's a very mean and nasty place, and I don't care how tough you are, it will beat you to your knees and keep you there permanently if you let it. You, me, or nobody is gonna hit as hard as life. But it ain't about how hard you hit, it's about how hard you can get hit and keep moving forward. How much you can take and keep moving forward. That's how winning is done!

Great public speakers I have witnessed have often used iconic lines from the world of movies. A dynamic senior partner I used to work with, asked his audience of the client sales team to sign up for his transformation programme. He went on to add, 'I request each of you to sign up wholeheartedly for this transformation programme. Why should you do it? Because I am going to make you an offer you cannot refuse.'

The reference to the iconic line from 'The Godfather' movie did bring a slight chuckle to the faces of many in the audience. He went on to narrate what benefits the programme will bring for each member through a combination of better career paths, market leadership positions and greater compensation.

I once saw a vice president, Sales address his team asking them not to take their leadership positions for granted. He was an avid tennis fan and used the following sporting reference,

> The 2011 Wimbledon quarter final had Roger Federer playing Jo-Wilfried Tsonga. Federer had won 16 Grand Slams till then. In that match, he won the first two sets. Wimbledon was his favourite surface. Federer had never lost from 2 sets up in his 250+ career Grand Slam matches[3] till then. Surely, the game would get over in the third or in the worst case, the fourth set. What do you think happened after that?

The VP was trying to convey the message that no matter who you are, you shouldn't take your leadership position for granted. And given his team members were avid tennis fans, they got the message clearly. Roger Federer went on to lose that match, on the back of 16 Grand Slams, on his favourite surface, in five sets. It was the first time in his career that he lost a match in five sets after being two sets up.

How else can you engage your audience using popular culture references?

If you are trying to get your leadership team to focus on the future, pull out any episode of the future-centric dark comedy,

---

[3] As a Federer fan, I was heartbroken. Incredible match to be honest: https://www.atptour.com/en/news/flashback-tsonga-federer-2011-wimbledon

Black Mirror and ask them what do they see in the future that doesn't exist today? And how long do you think we will take to get there? As the disturbing series will showcase, the dark future isn't far away.

If you want to get your leadership team to appreciate that the next generation, Gen Z, is completely different in their way of thinking, show them the trailers of *Euphoria*, *Elite* or *Sex Education* and ask them to interpret what they just witnessed. I can say with some conviction that a group of 45 plus-year olds will look at those trailers in complete horror. To be honest, some of those trailers can seem a little extreme but when you try to understand how the next generation thinks, the reality isn't far from what is shown in them. I would urge you to watch those trailers too. Without judgement.

USE COLOURS, IMAGES AND METAPHORS

When you are speaking to an audience, what do you think should matter to them? Take a guess.

Obviously, your words should be the most important. Goes without saying. Maybe your voice quality and modulation after that. The least should be your body language. Any rational mind, including mine, would say this. However, research indicates the exact opposite.

As per Professor Albert Mehrabian, a researcher of body language, 55 per cent of communication is through body language, 38 per cent is through our voice and only 7 per cent is through the actual words said. Let me put this number into perspective for you. You might be reciting a nursery rhyme to a group of CEOs but if you recite it properly with the right body language and the right voice modulation, there is a 90 per cent chance you might get away with it. In case this sounds ridiculous to you, ask yourself, how many people across the world are obsessed with politicians who lie blatantly and advocate killing someone else? If you notice very carefully, such politicians have outstanding voice modulation, delivery, pauses and body language.

Should this surprise you? It actually shouldn't. We have discussed in Chapter 3 titled 'How Does Hollywood Use Storytelling' and in Chapter 10 titled 'Making Elements Stick' that 'Colours, Images and Metaphors' have an incredible role in effective communication. While speaking, these elements manifest through the body language and voice modulation of the speaker.

Now, there is an infinite body of research and recommendations that has been made on body language and voice modulation. I will write about the top 3 irritants that you should completely avoid or master to become an exceptional orator. These are mistakes I have personally made in my corporate career.

Individually, I have always found it difficult to stand in one place and speak. Somehow, with the energy and the adrenaline generated while addressing an audience, I always want to move around. I once moved around by walking to the front and then walking to the back of the stage. The audience was completely confused when I said, 'I want your support in making this programme a success', as I started walking back away from the audience. Imagine a presenter asking for your support and walking back away from you. Over time, I have slowly started walking across from left to right and making eye contact with members of the audience. It works!

MY HANDS! I have been told so many times that I need to work on my body posture. There are coaches who have advised me to use my hands appropriately while speaking and not let them dangle like loose branches of a tree. If you are an expert, you will use your hands to support your arguments. For instance, if you are saying, inflation will rise, you will lift your right hand up. If you are saying, my third argument, you will show three fingers to an audience. I have felt extremely uncomfortable, and some of you may do too, to do these theatrics with my hands. As a compromise, I carry around an object in my hand these days. A book, a marker or sometimes even the speaker notes. While I do understand the audience gets distracted by it, still it is better than my hands dangling like two loose branches of a tree with no place to go.

I have repeatedly highlighted the role of colour while addressing an audience. In case you want to communicate about a necessary transformation that is disruptive and painful, a black and navy blue suit is the way to go. If you want to communicate about something optimistic and fun, go with lighter pastel shades. If you want to address a group of toddlers, try dressing up as Batman. You will have them hooked. And the golden rule, the audience, whether it is a toddler or a CEO, will always notice your shoes.

Of the many mistakes I have made while speaking, the one mistake I have never made, thankfully, is reading out of slides. In my view, this is totally criminal and absolutely unacceptable. The last thing you want your audience to do is to focus on your slides while they completely ignore you. And if you are saying the same thing as the slide, they honestly don't need you. One of the partners I worked with in consulting was repeatedly guilty of this trait. He was scared when the audience focussed on him. It was as if the slides had crippled him completely instead of being an aid for him to deliver an impactful presentation. He could never say anything other than what was written on the slide.

Some of us always wondered how he became a partner in the first place.

EMBRACE MINIMALISM

In a TEDx talk given by David Phillips on '110 techniques of communication and public speaking', the speaker after analysing over 5000 public speakers across the world mentions, 'you take a step forward towards your audience, you increase their focus towards you. You change the pace of what you are saying, you increase your audience's focus towards you. By lowering your voice, you get anticipation from your audience. If you pause, your audience gives you undivided attention.'

I was once trained by an Australian coach in leadership communication and her biggest advice to me and in her words to everyone she has trained the world over, is to 'SLOW DOWN'. She gave us a very interesting exercise. She asked us to pick any slide we have made and present that slide within 2 minutes to the audience in the room. We could not cross 2 minutes under any cost. Naturally, all of us tried to maximize our messages and data points in those 2 minutes by cramming everything into it.

Then she made us do an exercise where she asked us to use exactly half the number of sentences and present the same slide in 2 minutes. Naturally, we spoke slower with more pauses. Interestingly, the difference in impact was massive. Not just in sheer delivery but even with the sentences. The communication besides being extremely impactful was crisp and to the point. All unnecessary words and phrases were intuitively dropped. I would strongly urge you to try this exercise at home or with a friend in the office. Once you are comfortable, you should practice this exercise before every major presentation. Do a dry run of your presentation once and try saying the exact messages with half the sentences. I do it. It works like magic.

While delivering speeches in public, the slower you speak, the more impressive you become. The more minimalistic you are with words, the more impact you create. Do remember from the study quoted in the earlier pages that 38 per cent of your communication is vocal implying the way you speak matters more than the words you use. If you have ever been to a Buddhist monastery and interacted with the monks, your mind will be hooked on everything they are saying. Not just because of their wise words, but because they speak slowly and with abundant silence between their words. I have consciously tried to slow down my pace of speaking by over-pronouncing each word and taking conscious pauses in between. It takes time to get used to it. The silence is uncomfortable. But in this case, every small pause you take is a giant leap in your speaking capabilities.

The other minimalistic trick you should employ is not to speak for too long. What is a good length for a speech if you are presenting? If you look at TED speeches, they are all in the range of ten to fifteen minutes. In my view, you should never cross 20 minutes as Guy Kawasaki also says. After that, you are losing the audience's attention. I strongly believe 20 minutes is realistic even in corporate circles. It is only a mindset that holds us back.

The other big question people have is, should you write and memorize your speeches? After all, practice makes a person perfect. In a *Harvard Business Review* article titled, 'Stop Scripting Your Speeches',[4] the author highlights 'that writing, reading, and certainly memorizing a word-for-word speech is actually one of the most destructive and counterproductive tactics you can take as a presenter.'

How should you go about it then? Let us move to the next section.

FOLLOW RULE OF 3

Main idea I want to communicate? Women's cricket in India can become a global sport with the right level of support and investment.

---

[4] The link to the *Harvard Business Review* article: https://hbr.org/2021/01/stop-scripting-your-speeches

Support required? Three main levers—infrastructure funding, education campaign to change societal views towards young girls playing cricket and bringing in women coaches

#1: Infrastructure funding
- Amount of 100 million dollars
- How is Australia doing it?
- Mechanism of lending and advertising required

#2: Change societal perception
- Instagram or TikTok campaign
- Partner with schools
- Narrate the story of how Brazil encouraged young women to pick up football

#3: Bring in women coaches
- Parents get uncomfortable with male coaches
- Highlight coaching plan of bringing in coaches from Europe
- Coaching leadership institute to be set up to build domestic women coaches

Anecdote to start: My neighbour's child, Anita, 7, holds a cricket bat in the narrow lanes of Mumbai. She hopes to have breakfast with legendary cricketer Sachin Tendulkar someday.

Nested Anecdote to end: My neighbour's child, Anita wanted to have breakfast with Sachin Tendulkar. A day might not be far away when Sachin Tendulkar reaches out for Anita's autograph.

The above set of notes is exactly how I plan a speech. The broad skeleton is written in terms of the main idea, the 3 supporting arguments, an anecdote at the start and an anecdote at the end. I rehearse this once in my mind in terms of how I am going to narrate it and in my second practice run, can I narrate this with half the sentences?

Which principles of storytelling are being followed in this skeleton?

Power of anecdote to start? Yes.

Power of Nested Anecdote to end? Yes.

Rule of 3? Yes.

Pyramid principle to get to the main idea fast? Yes.

Minimalistic communication? Yes.

Why does this structure work for me? Because the broad storyline is set and yet I have enough leeway to adapt to the stage. No one likes a presenter who is reading from a slide or a written speech. Sometimes you need to say more or say less, say faster or say slower, say in a higher pitch or say in a lower pitch, by watching the members of your audience very closely.

Where can you use this rule of 3 for speaking?

In a boardroom? Yes.

Addressing your employees in a large forum? Yes.

Creating a video for your YouTube channel? Yes.

Proposing to your partner? PLEASE!

Preparing for your appraisal? For heaven's sake, No!

WALK ON

I said at the beginning of this chapter that becoming a master orator is a lifelong journey. It is much easier to write about (Figure 12.1) it than to practice it in real life. But there are ways to learn about becoming a master orator. There are books you can read, like this one you are currently reading or *Talk like Ted*. My personal recommendation is that each of you, in case you want to become a master orator, start a YouTube channel and make videos on a topic of your interest.

Facing the camera, even a mobile phone, is a scary experience and as you keep shooting more videos, your natural growth and comfort will make you an excellent orator. Also, to let you know, the first videos that you shoot need not be made public to the world. Only after you are comfortable, maybe you can release your videos to the outside world. But in my view, that is the easiest way to practice your art regularly.

An interesting avenue to becoming a great orator is also to teach at the local school or college on a topic that you are comfortable with. Young children or teenagers can be brutal as an audience and will force you to improve every day. If you are daring enough, make a teenager present to his batchmates and see how amazing they are at communicating with their community. There are so many lessons to learn from them.

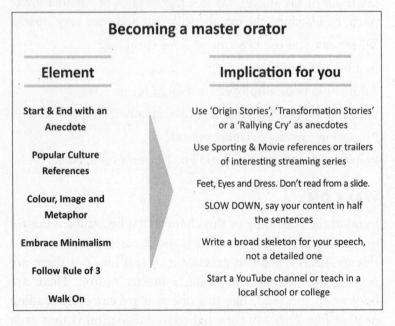

Becoming a master orator	
Element	**Implication for you**
Start & End with an Anecdote	Use 'Origin Stories', 'Transformation Stories' or a 'Rallying Cry' as anecdotes
Popular Culture References	Use Sporting & Movie references or trailers of interesting streaming series
	Feet, Eyes and Dress. Don't read from a slide.
Colour, Image and Metaphor	SLOW DOWN, say your content in half the sentences
Embrace Minimalism	Write a broad skeleton for your speech, not a detailed one
Follow Rule of 3	Start a YouTube channel or teach in a local school or college
Walk On	

Figure 12.1: Become a Master Orator via Storytelling

Why do you want this job?
Because I am passionate about not
starving to death.

A meme on the internet

Resume: Short fiction story
bearing no resemblance to actual events
or persons, living or dead.

Again, off the internet. Where else?

CHAPTER 13

EXCELLING IN INTERVIEWS

To say that succeeding in interviews is an important activity in your career is like saying you need to dance well to be an Instagram influencer. An interview, while obvious, is going to be the gateway to a hallowed opportunity, a dream career and an exit route from your present tormenting boss. The first step to getting an interview is to craft a version of the document you wish you actually were, which is your resume.

In this chapter, I will leverage my decade plus-long career in recruitment across management institutes and roles at leadership levels and my learnings from the same. In case you didn't get the above line, I will help you do slightly better at interviews and in framing your resume using the principles of storytelling.

How does storytelling help you in attending an interview and getting shortlisted? It is simple, because it makes you STAND OUT amid the noise. Especially when some portion of the process is now becoming virtual and the number of applicants for any post is increasing dramatically. And how does storytelling make you stand out? Well again, it is a chemical process. It makes you release the right set of chemicals in the interviewer's mind. As we will see in the subsequent pages.

Also, there is enough research from *Harvard Business Review* on this topic. I can share the links of heavy academic papers[1] with you but you should rather take my word that storytelling

---

[1] For the nerd in you, you can read this piece in *Harvard Business Review*. Although this piece is very well written - https://hbr.org/2021/05/the-key-to-landing-your-next-job-storytelling

works during the interview process and move on to learn the practical applications rather than reading through a highly intellectual piece of research for the next 2 days. And you will arrive at the same conclusion which I am telling you now that storytelling helps during the interview process.

Before we get into the business side of things, I have always been asked what do I look for while hiring candidates from entry to leadership roles.

Skillset? Yes.

Culture Fit? Yes.

Experience? Yes.

Temperament? Yes.

All of the above, definitely.

However, I have always resonated very strongly with the Google airport principle. Will I be comfortable with this person if I was stuck with him or her at an airport for a long period of time? While there are some who denounce this theory and some who vouch for it, I have always felt this theory implicitly works.

In the next few pages, in line with the 'Rule of 3', I am going to speak about 3 storytelling applications while interviewing for your dream job and 3 storytelling applications while creating your dream resume. To be honest, there can be many more applications, but I will focus on the top 3 which you can leverage immediately.

If I tell you every storytelling application in this book, will I be able to write my next book? How will I ever make money from you in the future?

TELL ME SOMETHING ABOUT YOURSELF

The first question you are always asked, in most interviews, is to tell the interviewer something about yourself. After having asked this question, maybe over 1,000 times, the nerd in me has programmed the elements of a standard answer.

<I have studied at X>

<I have been working for Y years at A, B and C>

<I have worked in the areas of A, B, C and D>

<Outside work, my hobbies include travelling, watching web series and reading>

To be honest, there is nothing wrong with this structure but if thousands of people are saying broadly the same thing, then your brain sort of gets bored. Notice in the first three lines, variables are used but in the last line, the hobbies are largely the same. I have seen a remarkable number of people list the same set of hobbies in their 'tell me something about yourself'.

How can you use storytelling to make this a lot more attractive? Let me give you 3 illustrations.

Outside work, I like to play cricket. I am a leg spin bowler. Over the last 12 months, I have been trying to learn to bowl the flipper.

Outside work, I like to read. I have been reading Sandeep Das' book on storytelling. I think his writing is very pop-culture-centric while being highly insightful.

Outside work, I love watching movies. I have been watching all of Leonardo DiCaprio's movies over the last 3 months. My favourites are *The Wolf of Wall Street* and *Shutter Island*.

What do you think happens when the last line of your introduction details your hobby like the statements above? Well, the interviewer is highly intrigued because he or she is not used to being given such answers.

Naturally, the next two questions are as follows,

Who is your favourite leg spinner? Can you bowl the googly?

I love Sandeep Das' books too. His YouTube channel is really great. (This is called shameless organic advertising)

I am a Christian Bale fan, not so much a DiCaprio fan. Did you like the Batman franchise?

As a result, the first 5 minutes of the conversation is on a topic you are extremely comfortable with. In addition, you are coming off as an interesting personality to the interviewer. They would fundamentally like to speak to you a little more. You are releasing the right set of chemicals in their brain.

What principle of storytelling is at play here?

It is how popular culture references resonate with everyone. Also, the power of anecdotes steps in. You are painting a vivid picture in your interviewer's brain. They are hooked. In addition, you are releasing dopamine in the minds of the interviewers and hence they are curious to talk to you about the same topic for some more time.

One small storytelling application, so many benefits.

DO YOU HAVE ANY QUESTIONS?

The most common interview question at the end of an interview is when the interviewer asks the candidate if he or she wants to know something about the role. Some people say no while some people ask a transactional question about the salary, role or location. Largely a 'Bleh Bleh' kind of interaction and exchange.

The most powerful question in my view you can ask is,

How has your experience been at this firm? What is your one highlight and one big challenge you have had to overcome?

I have seen myself and my fellow interviewers opening up to such a question and becoming very frank with the candidate rather than preaching about maintaining law and order on the planet Mars. A candidate also gets a very good sense of what he/she is signing up for with a very authentic and, more often than not, an interesting answer.

Why does this question work?

Often, it works because the candidate gets a real-life peek into the company they are trying to work for. Also, every interviewer is in love with their own story and feels good narrating about how they are better than all the Marvel superheroes.

Such a question often gives a candidate a 15–20 per cent bump in their chances at the end. Now, if you have had a bad interview, then such gimmickry doesn't help. But if your interview is on par with five other people, such gimmickry does help.

What is the storytelling principle that is at play here?

Remember how your mind largely remembers what happens at the end and mostly ignores what happened during the course of the journey. Exactly, that is being played out. The brain remembers the good vibe at the end of the interview and a few interesting highs during the course of the interview.

TELL ME THIS ONE TIME WHEN YOU SAVED EARTH FROM AN ALIEN STRIKE?

One of the most irritating set of questions is along the lines of 'Tell me this one time when you showed this leadership characteristic'. Whenever I was asked this question or was asked by HR to ask this question, I was reminded of this very irritating character 'Janice' from the hit series *Friends* who seemed to be screaming in my ear in her irritating, high-pitched voice. In case you don't recollect her, Janice is the 'Oh My God' lady from *Friends*.

Although irritating, these questions are necessary and can get boring for the candidate and the interviewer. However, you can use the principles of storytelling to make this experience a tad more pleasant.

The structure for such a narrative should be along the following lines,

Step 1: Define the problem

Step 2: What were the challenges?

Step 3: What was the struggle and what were the failures involved?

Step 4: How did you resolve it and succeed?

Note from Chapter 3 titled 'How Does Hollywood Use Storytelling', this is the basic structure in which every movie script is written. Every movie. Let me give you a few examples.

Tell me about a time you set a goal and achieved it.

<Problem> I have always aspired to be the author of a book

<Challenge> This is despite the fact that I have never written earlier in my life. I have no formal training in writing. And I didn't know anyone who had written a book.

<Struggle and Failure> I wanted to write a book of travelogues. I wrote for 4–6 hours every weekend and prepared the first draft. I sent it to a few friends. They didn't like it. So I rewrote major portions of the book to make it tighter. During my second draft, I did feel the book of travelogues was written by an amateur. So I went through tons of videos on YouTube on how to write a great travelogue. After going through online training for 6 months, I rewrote the manuscript.

<Resolution> I was very happy when I saw the first copy of my book after writing for 4–6 hours every weekend over a period of 3 years. It is the greatest feeling in the world to hold the first copy of your book in your hand.

To be honest, as you will agree, this is an extremely powerful story. Because it follows the standard movie script!

Let's do another one. A slightly more difficult one.

Tell me about a time when you had to fire someone.

<Problem> I was a people leader for the first time a few years ago. And given the performance framework was a bell curve, we had to let the bottom 5–10 per cent who were not meeting the minimum benchmark go.

<Challenge> It was difficult as it was the first time I was going to fire someone. To be fair, it wasn't as if we hadn't given this person feedback throughout the year. But somehow, this person, who had been employed there for many years, had started taking it lightly. It was going to be difficult as he was someone I knew more than just as a reportee.

<Struggle and Failure> Before the formal evaluation was out, I did try to give him a polite nudge and asked him to move out as a friend. He didn't take the hint. The first formal conversation, I had with him in the presence of HR, didn't go well. He erupted and became very aggressive and passionate. It wasn't that any of what we said was new to him. But he didn't take it well. We requested him to digest the news and come back for a follow-up conversation the next week. Thankfully, he had calmed down and that went much better.

<Resolution> It is never easy to let someone go. But when he put in his papers, we did give him a great farewell and internally, we spread the word that he left on his own rather than us pushing him out.

What storytelling principles are at play here?

All of what we discussed in Chapter 3 titled 'How Does Hollywood Use Storytelling' is being played out in front of you. The principles of tight problem definition, understanding challenges, depicting struggles and the resolution. In addition, with the vivid description, you want to hear more. Enter the chemical dopamine. You feel bad for the person being fired. Enter oxytocin. You are also wondering how you could do that firing differently. Your whole brain is hooked.

Let's move on to polishing your resume.

MINIMALISM ALL THE WAY

The single biggest principle that can be used to make your resume more attractive is minimalism. Remember from Chapter 3 titled 'How Does Hollywood Use Storytelling' on how movie editors and authors use minimalism—they delete 5 seconds of the movie or one paragraph from their book and check if the script falls flat. Only if the script falls flat is that deleted portion inserted back because it is seen as essential. Or else, it is seen as flab and removed. To be fair, I am not sure if I have applied the minimalistic principle to the book that you are currently reading.

Why does minimalism work? Because your brain is lazy. It wants to be fed with what is most important and it wants to form a pattern with the least amount of effort. Minimalism makes the necessary point with the least amount of information and effort.

As an interviewer, the single biggest truth is that no one spends more than 30–45 seconds on each resume. Remember that number, 30–45 seconds. If anyone tells you anything else, they are, for the lack of a better word, lying.

As a candidate, how do you use this principle of storytelling and minimalism to make your resume more attractive?

An interesting way to tackle your resume is to keep the high-impact sections first. This is primarily for younger professionals who can easily speak about education, work experience, internships and projects at their educational institute or student club activities. Given, an interviewer has only 30 seconds, start with the section that is the strongest. However, this might not apply to people with more than a few years of experience as your work experience has to be the first section.

I think the most important application of this principle is to make the first section an 'Executive Summary' where you highlight the 4–5 key points you would want your interviewer to know. It can have one line about your education, one line about the companies you have worked at, one line about your skill sets, one line about your awards and recognitions and one line about your hobbies. Think of this as a 'Tell me something about yourself' in a written form. I strongly advocate a video resume where this executive summary is spoken about and sent to the recruiter. It adds tremendous value to an individual's chances given the TikTok shorts and Instagram-reels-generation we live in.

There is an interesting tactic I have seen some modern professionals apply. They pick three key words which they think captures the spirit of their resume and write those words against their name at the top. For instance,

Sandeep Das—Leader, Strategist and Author

In a way, these 3 words are supposed to capture the essence of your resume. The storytelling principles at play are the 'Rule of 3', the 'Pyramid Principle' and 'Minimalism'. Personally, I have a mixed view on whether this approach works or not. Far too many candidates might use fancy words like 'innovator', 'consumer-centric' or 'entrepreneur' against their names thereby making someone with a genuine case seem redundant.

There are many more hygiene aspects like cutting down on unnecessary lines and jargons to make the resume reader friendly, using a large font, maybe colouring the background of your resume to make it easier to read, writing each point with the impact first and then the role. And finally sticking to one page no matter how special your life has been.

I am sure you know all of this already and I won't waste any paper on this.

In the spirit of 'minimalism' and given your brain is lazy, here are the few points you should remember (Figure 13.1) before you move on to the next chapter.

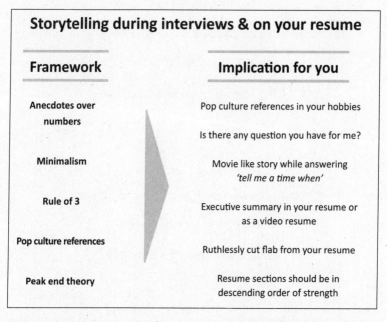

Storytelling during interviews & on your resume

Framework	Implication for you
Anecdotes over numbers	Pop culture references in your hobbies
	Is there any question you have for me?
Minimalism	Movie like story while answering 'tell me a time when'
Rule of 3	Executive summary in your resume or as a video resume
Pop culture references	Ruthlessly cut flab from your resume
Peak end theory	Resume sections should be in descending order of strength

Figure 13.1: You Are Welcome. Your Lazy Minimalistic Brain Owes Me One

The problem with the rat race is even if you win,
you are still a rat.

Lily Tomlin, American actress

Do not underestimate your abilities.
That is your boss' job.

Unknown, from the internet

CHAPTER 14

CREATING YOUR PERSONAL BRAND

There is so much NOISE around all of us.

Open Instagram or TikTok or YouTube, and there are 50,000 reels or shorts ready to grab your attention. Open a TV channel and 100 brands are trying to vie for your attention. Open a job posting that you like and there are 25,000 people ready to apply for that role. Open an interesting person's profile on Tinder and that person has 500 other potential suitors.

Every stage of life is getting tougher. Earlier, if you came from a good Ivy League college, you had it a tad easier. Now, education matters but not that much. Everyone you come across in the office, at the gym or in your friend circle is building this narrative that they are trying to change the world. And leading that perfect life.

Some might find the above situation scary. Some might find it natural. I find it a tad scary. But there are a lot of opportunities.

Why do I say it? You will find out in the next two pages.

It is a no-brainer that you have to stand out amid this NOISE to become successful professionally. One of the reasons you are reading this book is to stand out amid this noise. The issue here is two-pronged—one is the sheer number of people who are competing with you, and the other is the quality of the narrative you have to compete with. Remember, everyone is trying to craft 'their own story'. After reading this book, even more so.

Like I said earlier, everyone is trying to sell motivation, everyone claims to be a great boss, everyone loves people, everyone loves ethics or everyone is trying to change the world. This, for lack of a better word, is toxic positivity or just inauthentic.

Amid all this noise and toxic positivity, if you have to stand out, you have to create a strong personal brand. A strong brand at work, a strong brand in your peer circles and a strong brand by leveraging social media. One of the key elements in creating that personal brand is to come across as trustworthy or authentic. So many people are pretending to be fake in their corporate lives. Being authentic, or your true self, can be an incredible weapon to establish your social domination.

You may ask, does authenticity REALLY matter? Why not just keep pretending to change the world?

A *Forbes* piece, titled 'Why 2022 is the year to be your authentic self', claims that leaders being authentic or their true self, can become better leaders. Nearly 80 per cent of employees believe authenticity improves the workplace besides generating more trust and higher levels of productivity.[1]

Another *Forbes* piece claims if you have to appeal to a Gen Z audience or the next generation, authenticity is the number one character trait they are looking for.[2]

[1] Being authentic can make you a better leader, https://www.forbes.com/sites/kevinkruse/2022/01/07/why-2022-is-the-year-to-be-your-authentic-self/?sh=145acf085047
[2] Increasing importance of authenticity while communicating to Generation Z: https://www.forbes.com/sites/forbescommunicationscouncil/2022/02/16/gen-z-is-rising-is-your-brand-strategy-ready/?sh=701700aa3cb0

Authenticity makes you human. It makes you not sound like a chatbot. It helps you connect. Authenticity helps you develop a one-to-one connection with potentially millions of future consumers.

How do you create a strong personal brand (refer Figure 14.1)? You obviously have to be good at your work.

How do you amplify that message? Social media is a goldmine or a powerhouse most people are sitting on. For corporate professionals, like most of you, who are reading this book, LinkedIn is the preferred channel. But the same principles are applicable across Twitter and even TikTok or YouTube.

Once you have identified the social media platform, how do you become a trusted personal brand or someone seen as an expert? By coming across as your authentic self and not your fake pretentious self in front of everyone.

Once you have identified the platform to be your authentic self, which is the single biggest element that will help you get to scale your messaging on social media in a trusted authentic

Figure 14.1: Importance of Storytelling to Drive Authenticity to Build Your Personal Brand

way? You should have guessed it by now. Given you are reading a book on storytelling, it has to be the answer.

In the modern world, everyone is an influencer. You have to influence someone—your peers, your bosses, your future recruiters, your audience. You are always trying to influence someone rather than bulldoze your message through. Recall from Chapter 7 titled 'Creating Legendary Consumer Brands', how brands are actively tapping into influencers to drive their messages.

But isn't talking about yourself and your achievements shameless bragging? Even if it is done via storytelling and is authentic.

BUILD AN OMNICHANNEL ECOSYSTEM

You might be under the impression after reading the previous two pages that personal branding equals storytelling on LinkedIn. Let me kill that notion for you.

A couple of years ago, I happened to get a chance to interact with Professor Steven Sonsino from London Business School. He, besides being a brilliant leadership coach, is also a best-selling author and a renowned keynote speaker. His words of advice to me on building a personal brand were exceptionally powerful and easy to execute. He recommended that in order to build a personal brand, you should have an omnichannel ecosystem and create content once and multiply it everywhere. Let me explain.

Say, your topic of expertise is the stock market, and you want to create content on where the markets might be headed in the next 3 months. Why don't you write a two-page blog about your outlook on the stock market and put it up on LinkedIn? Then, why don't you create three interesting tweets from your blog and put them on Twitter? Then, why don't you shoot a 5-minute video basis your blog from your mobile phone and put it up on your YouTube channel? Then, why don't you cut out interesting sections from that 5-minute video and release them as Instagram reels? Then, why don't you extract the audio from that 5-minute video and use it on your podcast channel on Spotify?

What you are essentially doing is creating a single piece of content once and reusing that across multiple different platforms. There are clear benefits to following this approach.

Each social media platform has its own audience, and if you cater to them through the same content but represented differently, it will help you get visibility to different segments of people. Also, from an effort perspective, this method is highly productive. How often should you do this? Ideally, one blog a fortnight if you are starting off and one blog a week if you have got used to this method.

Also, personal branding is not just restricted to having a good presence on social media. As Professor Steven Sonsino's career trajectory shows, there is a great opportunity for becoming a keynote speaker. If you are starting off, you can try speaking at your college and local schools and in course of time, move towards corporates or even events like TEDx. There is value in speaking at in-person events. There is human touch and the huge benefit of NETWORKING. Physical and digital together make for a true omnichannel experience. How often should you speak at events in person? In my view, ideally, once a quarter.

Also as Steven himself says, if you know a subject really well, write a book on it. Writing a book, a short one, is not as tough as it seems. If you have worked in digital marketing for about 5 years, you can think of writing a 150-page book on that. It will help your personal brand immensely. If you know the world of stock markets extremely well, you could probably release a booklet on how to succeed in the stock markets and touch upon the myths that exist. I strongly concur with this approach. Whatever stage of your life you are in, you should consider writing a book on a skill that you have a degree of mastery in. It will help you immensely in life. For instance, you are currently reading a book on a skill that I have practiced over a long period of time—Business Storytelling.

As we have seen in Chapter 6 titled, 'Becoming a Visionary Entrepreneur', entrepreneurs are actively creating their personal brands as a marketing tool to stand out amid the noise.

If you think personal branding is only to make yourself more visible, that is actually incorrect. If you brand yourself well, you open up multiple sources of revenue for yourself. For instance, influencers who have a presence in the range of 20,000–50, 000 followers, start getting brand campaigns for some niche brands. After clocking 4,000 hours and 1,000 subscribers on your YouTube channel, you can make money through YouTube ads. You might get a couple of invites to industry panels and some speaking gigs. And so on. Personal branding besides helping you in your main career also opens up an alternate career.

If you want to know who is the gold standard when it comes to personal branding, there are a few names that come to my mind readily—Tony Robbins, Simon Sinek and Gary Vaynerchuk. However, there are also people like Elon Musk, Bill Gates and Sheryl Sandberg. Not to forget leading influencers in your part of the world. Not to forget the person in your office whom everyone seems to know and respect.

Where do you stand in this journey?

HAVE THE RIGHT MINDSET

In early 2020, I had a very interesting conversation with the editor of one of India's leading newspapers, a newspaper I currently write for. While intuitively I knew the importance of personal branding and tapping LinkedIn or YouTube to scale up my social expertise, I did look down upon people who flashed their achievements or marketed themselves a bit too much on social media. With my middle-class Asian upbringing, it was considered a huge taboo to talk about your own achievements. We were always taught to stay off the limelight and let our work speak for itself. By Karma. By God. By a spiritual superpower. I am sure if you have had an Asian upbringing, you will resonate with this theme of not marketing yourself aggressively and leaving it to your supervisor, your company or a greater power to take care of your career.

My editor heard me with a lot of patience. At the end of which, she said,

'If you want to become successful in life, you have to market yourself. If you don't market yourself, the world will not do it for you.'

It is an extremely profound statement. The biggest impediment in your personal branding journey might be your mindset. And to clear that up for you, PLEASE SHAMELESSLY SHOW OFF.

To be honest, I was really bad at LinkedIn when I decide to embrace this journey in early 2020. Not that I am great today, but my audience has swelled 30X during this period, and I am one of the more important thought leaders who is regularly quoted by the Indian media. My LinkedIn posts have garnered over 10 million views over this period. My YouTube videos have been seen over a million times. I have spoken at over 100 colleges and corporates. I have written over 150 pieces for leading Indian newspapers. The reason

I am bragging to you is because you can also undertake a similar ecosystem journey as mine. You can start at the same point I did a couple of years ago.

In this chapter, I am going to take you through how you can build a great personal brand across your ecosystem using the elements of storytelling. As you will notice, academic theory has been deliberately kept at a minimum in this chapter. What matters here is practical action, and this chapter has lots of it.

GET BASICS IN PLACE

Let us take LinkedIn as an example throughout the chapter although the same principles apply whether you are targeting YouTube, Instagram or Spotify. If you are looking to speak at an in-person conference, the principles mentioned in Chapter 12 titled 'Becoming a Master Orator' are fully applicable. But before we start, you should know that storytelling on its own is not the only way to scale up your brand on LinkedIn. You need to have a few basics in place. You need to post content regularly. If you are a newbie, you should write a blog once a fortnight and post content across your ecosystem as we discussed earlier. If you are more seasoned, you should write a blog every week and post content across your ecosystem around it regularly.

You have to engage with your community by replying to as many messages as you can. Recall from Chapter 7 titled 'Creating Legendary Consumer Brands' that for a brand, interacting with consumers is going to become a key differentiating factor in the future. You have to be factually accurate and not get into political fights or ugly debates on social media. My leader is better than your leader is a huge no–no.

Before we get into what works, let us start this discussion with what doesn't work when you are trying to build a personal brand using storytelling.

What kind of content doesn't work on LinkedIn? And similarly on YouTube, Twitter, Spotify or speaking at an in-person event? It is very simple. When your audience realizes you are being fake or are bluffing. Nothing erodes trust faster than being fake.

There are common posts on LinkedIn that a lot of wannabe influencers post to gain a few likes or subscribers. Following are some of them,

> I was going in for my dream interview. I met someone during the journey who was seemingly sick and needed help. I chose to give up the interview but sat with him till he felt better at the station. It turned out he was by interviewer's boss and I got that job. Karma always wins.

> I wanted to hire someone with 2–3 years of work experience for the role I was interviewing with. A fresher with no experience wanted to give that interview. I interviewed him and found the fresher to be really good. Despite no experience, I decided to invest in him and gave him the job. Today, after 2 years, he is a top performer with many reporting under him.

'I am a great people leader. I empower everyone who works under me. I ensure people get all weekends off. I promote my people faster than everyone else.'

What is wrong with the above content for LinkedIn? Besides being plagiarized in some way, they seem fake. Why do you think they seem fake?

They seem to be playing on common platitudes in life like karma or fairness or respect or decency or women empowerment. True, some people are genuine when they post such content, and somehow when you read their posts, you realize they are not bluffing.

WHAT IS YOUR NICHE?

If you recall Chapter 7 titled 'Creating Legendary Consumer Brands', we tapped into what brands stand for. Great brands always start with what they stand for. Coca-Cola wants to refresh the world. Amazon wants to be the most consumer-centric company in the world. Apple wants to create products that enrich people's daily lives.

As you are creating your own personal brand, ask yourself what is the niche you are trying to build for yourself. Like the 'Rule of 3' in storytelling says, identify 3 principles. Less than 3, your brain can't form a pattern. More than 3, it gets complex. More importantly, the principle of having a 'clear problem statement' is at play here. Recall from Chapter 3 titled 'How Does Hollywood Use Storytelling?', if you don't have a clear problem statement, the whole movie goes for a toss.

For instance, the three things I stand for are career skills, corporate strategy and alternate careers. If you see my own LinkedIn posts and my ecosystem, I comment on career skills like communication, networking, problem-solving and succeeding in interviews. As I have held leadership positions in consulting and FMCG, I comment on strategy in these two industries. Given my background in writing and speaking, I comment on alternate careers. Around 90 per cent of my posts revolve around these things.

If you look at Simon Sinek, renowned author and speaker with over six million followers on LinkedIn, he typically comments on leadership, the future of our world and motivation.

If you look at Bill Gates, co-founder of Microsoft and philan-thropist, with over 35 million followers on LinkedIn, he typically comments on technology, philanthropy and books.

What do you want to be known for and how can you build a brand around it? (Figure 14.2)

Figure 14.2: How Do You Build an Ecosystem for Your Personal Brand?

If you are in analytics, you could speak on analytics, consumer behaviour and probably technology.

If you are in strategy, you could speak about strategy, new business models and the future.

If you are in marketing, you can speak about emerging trends, consumer behaviour and brand purpose.

If you are a teacher in mathematics, you could speak about numbers, ease of education and real-world applications.

If you have a work experience of over two decades, you could speak about work culture, people management and the broader economy.

Pick what you want to be known for and then post content around those 3 pillars. It doesn't matter if someone else is also covering those 3 pillars. Like your DNA, everyone's experiences are unique. More importantly, the world has enough space for everyone to build their personal brands. Your 3 pillars need not be totally new to the world.

STORYTELLING TO CREATE CONTENT

A storytelling-oriented post that you create should follow the 3-part movie structure we looked at in Chapter 3 titled 'How Does Hollywood Use Storytelling'. A problem statement followed with the struggle followed by a resolution. You can leverage this principle while speaking about your mistakes, your failures, your learnings, your day-to-day opinions on current affairs and so on.

Talking about your failures and resultant learnings can showcase you as an authentic leader on social media. The reason for that is people only talk about their successes on social media and showcase their best and mostly fictional selves. However, your failures and resultant learnings are probably similar to the failures of millions of others, and when you speak about it, it resonates with millions of people. Recall from Chapter 6 titled 'Becoming a Visionary Entrepreneur' that talking about your failures generates oxytocin, the empathy chemical, in your audience, and they are hooked onto your narrative. This is why upcoming entrepreneurs always weave in anecdotes about their failures during any interview or while addressing an audience.

Gary Vaynerchuk, renewed author and influencer, with over five million followers follows this principle quite often. In the following post, he speaks on the importance of thinking long term rather than a lucrative short-term opportunity.

> One of my biggest career mistakes was moving Wine Library TV from YouTube to Viddler. They gave me a big chunk of the company to move over there, and I took the short-term bag instead of building attention on YouTube. Humongous

mistake. I could have had millions more subscribers had I stayed on YouTube in 2007–2011, but I didn't. More importantly, I didn't cry about it or dwell. I adjusted, moved forward and never made that same mistake again. The lesson? When it comes to brand building and entrepreneurship, always think in the macro or long-term over short-term. It's so fun to be a marathon runner in a world full of sprinters.

I posted the following message about failing early in life, but it turned out to be a blessing in disguise.

Your greatest failure in life is often the greatest blessing from above. My final placements at IIM Bangalore were a complete disaster. From starting my interview with the best company on campus, it took me over 25 rejections to just get a job. I had missed the road to corporate success and status. Most people, including me to a certain extent, had written myself off completely. The dog was dead even before he had barked. During that time, final placements in IIMs were hyped beyond belief.

What that experience did was, given I was so badly beaten that I didn't even deserve to be a part of the rat race and hence I had no burden of expectations from anyone. Hence, I pursued my desire to write and speak in the background without any pressure or burden. Did this for a period of 10 years without any pressure.

When people ask me today how I managed to succeed in my writing and speaking career so well, it has to be with the greatest failure in my life. While I wasn't able to connect the dots in 2009, there was clearly someone above who could see the road ahead.

In fact, I see so many of my 'successful' peers dying to lead a life on their own terms but trapped in the endless cycle of promotions, salary comparisons and job titles.

Someday when I meet the big person above and she/he asks me, what is the biggest blessing you received in your life, I will wholeheartedly say the disastrous final placements at IIM Bangalore! That is the day, you truly set me up for lifelong success!

When you speak about your failures, they need not be about incidents from life. They can be purely technical.

If you are a designer, you can speak about how your system design didn't incorporate the theory of constraints and, as a result, you had resultant leakage.

If you are a programmer, you can speak about how you weren't leveraging templates adequately while debugging when you started and how you incorporated that later.

If you are a B2B sales professional, you can speak about how you were hesitant to clarify the scope of the project explicitly and how it snowballed into a massive scope creep later on.

While some of the above posts are long, ideally, the posts should be minimalistic, meaning you should explain them in the fewest words possible.

One of the best storytelling techniques is to bring out real-world moving anecdotes to drive a larger message of struggle, perseverance and hope. There are few pages that do extremely well—Humans of New York or Humans of Bombay. They leverage the power of anecdotes generating the right set of chemicals in your brain and the 3-part movie structure. There have been numerous campaigns online that have been leveraged to generate funds for someone's treatment or fill in a young student's fees. As an influencer, if you can champion such causes, they are good, not just for the world but even to help your public image.

You can also leverage the principle of storytelling by bringing in the element of popular culture references. In Chapter 7 titled, 'Creating Legendary Consumer Brands', we saw how brands leverage moment marketing by commenting on the issue of the day. Remember the cute memes by leading Indian dairy brand Amul?

It is an extremely interesting way of connecting real-time with an audience and sharing your true opinions. When it comes to moments of the day, I comment on corporate results, cricket match scores and lifestyle elements like movies or a new restaurant or cuisine. Building a personal brand is not just about giving earth-shattering wisdom but by truly being yourself on the day-to-day issues in people's lives.

A group of CEOs in India, like Vivek Gambhir (ex-Godrej Consumer Products Limited and now CEO at boAt) and Ashok Ramaswamy (CEO and President at Schindler India), speak and write openly on what is at the top of their minds with respect to corporate India and their blogs, podcasts, reels and videos get great coverage.

The 'Rule of 3' also plays out while building a narrative. Leading Indian influencer, Raj Shamani, with a social media footprint of over two million, leverages the power of 3 by posting about 3 books he likes, 3 interesting news on a particular day or 3 reasons why a particular corporate move happened. His posts are short and crisp and generate great coverage. He is extremely successful across YouTube, Instagram, Twitter and LinkedIn.

So should all your posts be about your failures, learnings and commentary on moments of the day? Not necessarily.

You have to ensure that you stick to the core of the 3 pillars you have identified. Also, there is a problem with excessive motivation and sob stories. You have to serve technical content where your audience also sees value.

However, at the end of the day, there is a certain amount of self-promotion we all have to do. We have to talk about our promotions and our degrees and showcase our knowledge to the outside world. How you balance that self-promotion while bringing your true self to the outside world is what will define your success.

In my case, I keep it at 30 per cent content for self-promotion and about 70 per cent content to bring forward my authentic self to my community. You will have to figure out what works best for you.

And I have left the most important point till the end. 'Creating Your Personal Brand' is a lifelong journey, and it needs an hour of effort every day. In my view, this is the one investment that will give you disproportionate rewards in your life.

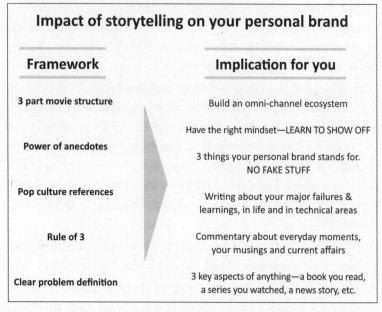

Impact of storytelling on your personal brand

Framework	Implication for you
3 part movie structure	Build an omni-channel ecosystem
	Have the right mindset—LEARN TO SHOW OFF
Power of anecdotes	3 things your personal brand stands for. NO FAKE STUFF
Pop culture references	Writing about your major failures & learnings, in life and in technical areas
Rule of 3	Commentary about everyday moments, your musings and current affairs
Clear problem definition	3 key aspects of anything—a book you read, a series you watched, a news story, etc.

Figure 14.3: Impact of Storytelling on Your Personal Brand

*If all the economists were laid end to end,
they'd never reach a conclusion.*

George Bernard Shaw, Winner of the
Nobel Prize in Literature

*It is good to have an end to journey forward;
but it is the journey that matters, in the end.*

Ernest Hemingway, American novelist

*Till the full stop doesn't come, the
sentence is not complete.*

Mahendra Singh Dhoni, legendary Indian cricketer

CONCLUSION
The Final Story

So we have reached the last part of this book. At least, I have had a fantastic time writing this book. I am quite sure you must have had an amazing time reading it too. If you have reached till this point, I am sure you MUST have had one.

As we finish, I should emphasize again that storytelling will be the most important skill you will need to succeed in your lives over the next few decades. It is the single most important reason you are alive and reading this book. It is also important to realize that this book doesn't have all the answers to storytelling. In fact, no book can ever have.

Storytelling is an art and a science and it takes a lifetime to master it. This book is Step 1 in your very long journey to becoming a master storyteller. Some of you might ask the question—how can you become better at storytelling. Well, the obvious way is to practice more in your life with the principles mentioned in this book.

There are other resources that you can also use daily to become a better storyteller every day. In the next few paragraphs, I will write about my own regimen for trying to become a better storyteller every day.

MY OWN STORYTELLING REGIMEN

Nothing has taught me more about storytelling than the world of movies and hit television and streaming series. As a policy, I watch, without fail, an hour of television or streaming series every day. There is no greater education in life that I have received.

Historically, I have loved *The Mentalist, How to Get Away with Murder, Peaky Blinders, Squid Games, Billions, House,* etc. Although I could never get addicted to the *Game of Thrones*. I know, I am weird!

As I write this chapter, I am currently going to start watching *The Severance* and *Chernobyl*.

No one is a better storytelling teacher than Christopher Nolan. I have watched his movies again and again trying to understand plot and dialogue nuances. I would strongly recommend this exercise for anyone keen on pursuing this art with utmost devotion. My favourite Christopher Nolan movies have always been the Batman franchise and *The Prestige*. Throughout my career, I have used Batman as the most common popular culture reference with CXOs and it has always worked out.

A particular genre of movies and books that are very well written from a storytelling perspective are documentaries or biographies. I loved *The Last Dance, Tiger* (Ace golfer Tiger Woods' biography), *Steve Jobs, Moneyball,* etc. I would strongly recommend each of you to watch *The Last Dance*. It is a breathtaking piece of storytelling as it documents the journey of legendary basketball player Michael Jordan and how he and his team, Chicago Bulls, win their sixth NBA title against all odds.

There are certain books that are great associated reads as part of storytelling. I strongly recommend *Sapiens, Nudge* and *The Billionaire's Apprentice*. Not to forget *Billion Dollar Whale* which is a story about how Jho Low, a Malaysian playboy, went on to con the global financial system and was also one of the producers of the fantastic movie, *The Wolf of Wall Street*. An ironic but great story.

Here is a suggestion which you might be very surprised with. The best storytellers are often associated with sports entertainment, think of WWE or World Wrestling Entertainment. A great piece of storytelling, if you are keen, is to watch the build up to the match between The Undertaker and Shawn Michaels as part of the 'Career versus Streak' match.

It is one of the great pieces of storytelling with an outstanding background music score (the track's name is 'Running Up That Hill'). The match is between two legends. If Undertaker loses, his unbeaten streak at the flagship event of WWE, WrestleMania, is over. If Shawn Michaels loses, his storied career comes to an end. There is conflict, drama and emotion and the promo video for the match is outstanding storytelling. You can watch it on YouTube.

I do believe podcasts because of their format inherently deploy great storytelling. Pick any one that you might like. You will intuitively see the principles mentioned in this book come to life. I listen to the podcasts by the *Wall Street Journal* and *The Economist* every day.

There are varied ways in which you can watch storytelling in all its might. If you have a 6-year-old at home, ask him or her 'how their day was?' And you will be amazed at how good children are at natural storytelling. It is a little unfortunate that, as a society, we mess up their natural skillset as they enter adulthood.

Also, if you are lucky enough to have grandparents around, ask them about 'their first day in college', 'their first day at work', 'their struggles in life' or 'their happiest days'. Watch their inner Christopher Nolan take centre stage. It is fascinating to see that children and grandparents are excellent storytellers. It is only people like you and me, who are working, who are not as good with storytelling despite the fact that our livelihood depends on it. One of the many ironies of life.

I have always found the product launches by Apple to have great stories consciously built into them. They have somehow mastered the art of storytelling in all their products. Their launch videos showcase storytelling. Their product ads showcase storytelling. Not to be left behind, Tesla's boss and controversial genius, Elon Musk, is an excellent storyteller on Twitter.

When in doubt, follow TED Talks. You won't go wrong with it. All of their videos have storytelling as the front and centre experience. If you consciously follow TED Talks, you will see all the principles of this book come alive.

Also, you can follow an influencer like me on social media. As you can see, I don't like to show off my humility. To be honest, there are great stories everywhere. Listen to campaign speeches of politicians. Listen to leaders speaking about their journeys at networking events. Listen to Sheryl Sandberg as she speaks or writes. Read a comic strip of Calvin and Hobbes. Watch the stand-up comics, they are excellent at storytelling. It is up to you and me, how much we want to absorb from the world around us.

On a serious note, in line with the 'Rule of 3' and to get your personal branding journey started, why don't you write 3 things you learned or liked from this book on your social media. Besides helping me, which you obviously should, you can get started on your storytelling journey today.

If there are a few takeaways you should remember from this book, it has to be 'The 10 Golden Rules of Storytelling'. Read them one more time and hopefully not the last time.

THE 10 GOLDEN RULES OF STORYTELLING

#1: Storytelling is the main reason we as a species are alive today. It will be the #1 reason your corporation or start-up will be alive tomorrow. It is the single biggest skill set you will need. It will impact every aspect of your life, personal and professional.

#2: Storytelling is gripping because it releases certain chemicals in your brain. By knowing how to tactfully release those chemicals in your audience's brain, you can get people hooked on your message.

#3: Your brain judges an experience primarily by its ending rather than how long it takes or what happens in the middle. This finding is profound and has applications in so many areas.

#4: Your brain loves communication in 'groups of 3'. Less than 3, it can't form a pattern. More than 3, it becomes effort intensive for your brain.

#5: Your brain loves minimalistic communication as it is fundamentally lazy and has an entire body to run. Cut off all the flab.

#6: Your brain loves a powerful anecdote. It loves to visualize itself in that anecdote. It always chooses an anecdote over a number. A Nested Anecdote becomes incredibly powerful.

#7: Your brain loves a story provided the problem statement is clear. If the problem statement isn't clear, your brain treats the experience like a snooze fest.

#8: Your brain loves popular culture references. It immediately connects with what is commonly available to everyone. It just gets it. Also, never underestimate the power of symbols, metaphors and colour. It is often central to storytelling.

#9: While narrating a story, your brain loves the tension, the build-up or the challenges. In simple English, the 'why' is supremely important.

#10: And most importantly, reread these 9 principles mentioned above.

I would strongly suggest that you identify 3 applications of these principles as part of the chapters in Parts 2 and 3 of this book.

In any communication I make, I blindly follow 3 principles— being minimalistic, using anecdotes and popular culture references. It makes my communication stand out almost every time.

A FINAL TWIST

One of the most memorable chapters in this book has been the chapter where I write about storytelling principles you can learn from the world of movies. To refresh your memory, refer to the image in Figure C.1.

We discussed how a movie has 3 main acts. Act 1 where you define the problem. Act 2 where you increase the tension and Act 3 where you resolve the tension. We discussed the 'Rule of 3', clear problem definition, minimalism and the importance of the trivial element.

I also highlighted the role of the twist at the end. A twist at the end makes the entire movie so much more memorable. Remember how your brain loves a twist at the end and evaluates an entire experience by the end rather than the duration of the experience.

Like a good movie, a good book should also have a twist at the end.

Or else, what is the fun in reading?

And I am sure some of you have probably figured this out by now.

In case you haven't, this is how the twist in this book goes.

This book has been written in the same exact structure as the image of a typical movie script I wrote about. AND YOU, NOT I, WERE THE PROTAGONIST ALL ALONG!

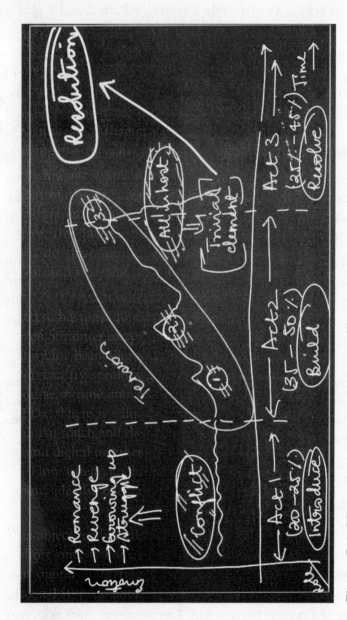

Figure C.1: How a Movie Script Is Generally Written

Act 1, Act 2 and Act 3? Tick

Problem statement definition? Tick

Defining the context? Tick

Increasing the tension? Tick

A trivial element? Tick

Resolving the problem? Tick

Twist at the end? A BIG TICK

Ask yourself,

What was the conflict?

How was the tension built?

What is the trivial element?

How did the conflict get resolved?

In case you are not sure, go through the table of contents and key chapters of this book again and look at it from the lens of the image in Figure P.1. It will become clear to you.

You are welcome :)